A DIAGNOSTIC STUDY OF THE CIVIL SERVICE IN INDONESIA

JANUARY 2021

ASIAN DEVELOPMENT BANK

 Creative Commons Attribution 3.0 IGO license (CC BY 3.0 IGO)

© 2021 Asian Development Bank
6 ADB Avenue, Mandaluyong City, 1550 Metro Manila, Philippines
Tel +63 2 8632 4444; Fax +63 2 8636 2444
www.adb.org

Some rights reserved. Published in 2021.

ISBN 978-92-9262-686-0 (print); 978-92-9262-687-7 (electronic); 978-92-9262-688-4 (ebook)
Publication Stock No. TCS210016-2
DOI: http://dx.doi.org/10.22617/TCS210016-2

The views expressed in this publication are those of the authors and do not necessarily reflect the views and policies of the Asian Development Bank (ADB) or its Board of Governors or the governments they represent.

ADB does not guarantee the accuracy of the data included in this publication and accepts no responsibility for any consequence of their use. The mention of specific companies or products of manufacturers does not imply that they are endorsed or recommended by ADB in preference to others of a similar nature that are not mentioned.

By making any designation of or reference to a particular territory or geographic area, or by using the term "country" in this document, ADB does not intend to make any judgments as to the legal or other status of any territory or area.

This work is available under the Creative Commons Attribution 3.0 IGO license (CC BY 3.0 IGO) https://creativecommons.org/licenses/by/3.0/igo/. By using the content of this publication, you agree to be bound by the terms of this license. For attribution, translations, adaptations, and permissions, please read the provisions and terms of use at https://www.adb.org/terms-use#openaccess.

This CC license does not apply to non-ADB copyright materials in this publication. If the material is attributed to another source, please contact the copyright owner or publisher of that source for permission to reproduce it. ADB cannot be held liable for any claims that arise as a result of your use of the material.

Please contact pubsmarketing@adb.org if you have questions or comments with respect to content, or if you wish to obtain copyright permission for your intended use that does not fall within these terms, or for permission to use the ADB logo.

Corrigenda to ADB publications may be found at http://www.adb.org/publications/corrigenda.

Notes:
In this publication, "$" refers to United States dollars.
ADB recognizes "China" as the People's Republic of China.

Cover design by Michael Cortes.

CONTENTS

Tables and Figures	iv
Foreword	vi
Acknowledgments	viii
Abbreviations	x
1. Introduction	1
2. Human Resources in Indonesia's Civil Service	3
3. Capacity and Skills	10
3.1. A Deeper Look at the Education Sector	27
3.2. The Role of Gender and Diversity	28
4. Governance and Institutional Context	33
4.1. Recruitment Process for Civil Service Applicants	33
4.2. Public Sector Performance, Corruption, and Clientelism	39
5. Recommendations and Conclusion	47
References	49

TABLES AND FIGURES

Tables

2.1	Number of Employees in National Civil Service Units, 2015	4
2.2	Number of Civil Servants by Level of Government, 2018	4
2.3	Total Number of Civil Servants (Including District Employees) by Province, 2018	5
2.4	Number of Civil Servants by Type, 2015	7
2.5	Indonesian Civil Servants by Age Bracket and Gender, 2018	9
3.1	Educational Attainment of Civil Servants by Gender, 2018	11
3.2	Educational Attainment of Civil Servants by Age Bracket, 2018	12
3.3	Education of All Civil Servants by Gender and Echelon Level, 2015	13
3.4	Education Level of Central Government Civil Servants by Echelon and Gender, 2015	13
3.5	Educational Level of Regional Civil Servants by Echelon and Gender, 2015	14
3.6	Average Educational Attainment by Echelon and Government Levels, 2015	14
3.7	Largest National Departments and Agencies by Education Level, 2015	15
3.8	Average Education Level of Civil Servants by Province, 2015	16
3.9	Top-10 District Governments by Average Education Level, 2015	17
3.10	Bottom-10 District Governments by Average Education Level, 2015	17
3.11	Performance of Civil Servants in Indonesia, 2018	22
3.12	Performance of Civil Servants in National Departments, 2018	23
3.13	Government Performance Indices	26
3.14	Share of Female Civil Servants by Echelon, 2015	29
3.15	Share of Religious Minority Civil Servants by Echelon, 2015	30
3.16	Top-10 National Departments by Share of Female Civil Servants, 2015	30
3.17	Bottom-10 National Departments by Share of Female Civil Servants, 2015	31
3.18	Top-10 Districts by Share of Female Civil Servants, 2015	31
3.19	Bottom-10 Districts by Share of Female Civil Servants, 2015	31
4.1	Echelon Levels in Indonesia's Civil Service	35
4.2	Civil Servants by Echelon Level, 2018	36
4.3	Civil Servants by Golongan (Rank), 2018	36
4.4	Golongan (Rank) by Age Bracket, 2018	37

Figures

2.1	Number of Civil Servants in Indonesia, 2009–2018	3
2.2	Share of Civil Servants by Government Level, 2009–2018	5
2.3	Civil Servants as a Percentage of the Local Population, 2015	6
2.4	Distribution of Midwives per 1,000 People, 2015	7
2.5	Distribution of Teachers per 1,000 People, 2015	7
2.6	Share of Civil Servants by Type, 2018	8
2.7	Job Types of Functional-Specific Civil Servants, 2015	8
2.8	Distribution of Civil Servants across Age Brackets, 2018	9
3.1	Indonesia's Civil Servants by Educational Attainment, 2018	11
3.3	Average Education Level of Medical Staff in Civil Service across Districts, 2015	18
3.2	Average Education Level of Civil Servants across Districts, 2015	18
3.4	Average Education Level of Teachers in Civil Service across Districts, 2015	19
3.5	Digital Competency of Governments, 2019	21
3.6	Professionalism Index Scores across District Governments, 2019	22
3.7	Open, Useful, and Reusable Government Data (OURdata) Index, 2018	25
3.8	Collection and Aggregation of Employee Performance Data, 2018	25
4.1	Distribution of Golongan (Rank) by Level of Government, 2018	37
4.2	Services Provision Index, 2003–2013	40
4.3	Births Attended by Skilled Staff, 2001–2012	40
4.6	Access to Safe Water, 2001–2013	41
4.4	School Enrollment, 2008–2012	41
4.5	Access to Safe Sanitation, 2001–2013	41
4.8	Access to Public Services across Institutions, 2006, 2011, and 2016	42
4.7	Poverty per Capita, 2002–2013	42
4.9	Level of Trust across Institutions in Indonesia in 2006, 2011, and 2016	43
4.10	Level of Trust across Institutions in Indonesia in 2006, 2011, and 2016 (Alternative Breakdown)	43
4.11	Percentage of Births Attended by Skilled Staff, 2011	44
4.12	Perception of Government Corruption in Southeast Asia, 2018	46

FOREWORD

Civil servants are an integral part of successful and responsive governance. Governments, both in low- and high-income settings, are facing increasingly complex policy challenges and have to operate in a rapidly changing technological, economic, social, and political landscape.

To adapt to these challenges and environments, modern civil service organizations require a workforce of competent, dedicated, and mission-driven public servants. Civil servants are the key resources available to governments for improving public service delivery. Consequently, the composition and management of the civil service workforce is an important arena for policy reforms that aim to improve government performance. Solving complex challenges, leveraging new technologies to improve citizen–state interaction, catering to diverse and vulnerable populations, and increasing the transparency and legitimacy of government processes are impossible without an in-depth consideration of hiring, training, and management practices in the civil service.

Indonesia is an instructive case in point. Since the Reformasi period, which led to the embrace of democratic norms and institutions, Indonesia's civil service had to deal with several challenges and it has gone through substantial internal changes. Ranging from the hardships imposed during the Asian financial crisis, far-reaching decentralization reforms that upended the centralized structure of the bureaucracy, to the current public health challenges of the COVID-19 pandemic, Indonesia's civil servants have played a key role in the successes and failures of the Indonesian government over the last 20 years. Understanding why the Indonesian civil service has failed and how it has improved is crucial to establishing modern, accountable, and transparent governance in the future.

This report surveys the current state of the Indonesian civil service from a comprehensive, data-driven perspective. Drawing on data pertaining to the civil service's size and composition, public service delivery, and public opinion, it visualizes the current challenges facing Indonesia's bureaucracy. While progress has been made, there is much room for improvement for increasing the basic competencies of Indonesia's civil servants and mitigating substantial spatial heterogeneity in the presence and quality of the civil service across the Indonesian archipelago.

The Asian Development Bank team worked closely with the National Development Planning Agency (BAPPENAS), National Civil Service Agency (BKN), National Institute of Public Administration (LAN), and Ministry of Administrative and Bureaucratic Reform (MenPAN) to put together this diagnostic report of Indonesia's civil service. We hope that it will contribute to the Indonesian government's efforts at enhancing the quality of its public sector.

Ayako Inagaki
Director, Human and Social Sector Division
Southeast Asia Department
Asian Development Bank

ACKNOWLEDGMENTS

This report was prepared by Jan Pierskalla, an Associate Professor at Ohio State University, United States. Sameer Khatiwada, Social Sector Specialist at the Southeast Asia Department of the Asian Development Bank (ADB) and Emma Allen, Country Economist at ADB's Indonesia Resident Mission supervised the report and provided technical input. Ayako Inagaki, Director of ADB's Social Sector Division; Winfried F. Wicklein, Country Director of ADB's Indonesia Resident Mission; and Said Zaidansyah, Deputy Country Director of ADB's Indonesia Resident Mission provided guidance and support.

This study would not have been possible without support from the Government of Indonesia. We thank Slamet Soedarsono, Deputy for Politics, Law, Defence and Security at the National Development Planning Agency (BAPPENAS); Pungky Sumadi, Deputy for Population and Manpower, BAPPENAS; and Tatang Muttaqin, Director for the State Apparatus, BAPPENAS for their input. We are also grateful to Avanti Fontana, Special Advisor to the Chief of Staff, Office of the President (KSP) and Agus Sudrajat, Deputy for Research and Management Innovation, National Institute of Public Administration (LAN) for their valuable feedback to the ADB team.

We acknowledge the contribution of Bima Haria Wibisana, Head of the Civil Service Agency (BKN); Setiawan Wangsaatmaja, former Deputy for Human Resources Development at the Ministry of Administrative and Bureaucratic Reform (MenPAN); and Mudzakir, Secretary Deputy of Human Resources Apparatus at MenPAN.

The BAPPENAS workshop on 12 March 2020 brought together participants, including senior officials from KSP, LAN, and MenPAN, who engaged in a lively discussion on the preliminary findings of ADB's civil service diagnostic study, the role of the public sector, and the need for better acquisition and management of talent to deliver public goods and services.

Workshop discussants offered detailed and beneficial insights on civil service diagnostics: Eko Prasojo from the University of Indonesia; R. Siti Zuhro of the Indonesian Institute of Sciences; Agus Pramusinto, Chairman of the State Civil Apparatus Commission; Muhammad Taufiq, Deputy of Competency Development Policy of LAN; and Jaleswari Pramodhawardhani, Deputy of Politics, Law, Security and Human Rights at KSP.

Yanuar Nugroho, Center for Innovation Policy and Governance guided the ADB investment project team with regard to improving human capital development and talent management in Indonesia's civil services. His assistance was invaluable during the final phases of this report and contributed to the design of the talent management project.

ADB's governance group in the Sustainable Development and Climate Change Department (SDCC) reviewed this report—we are thankful to Bruno Carrasco, Chief of Governance, SDCC, and Claudia Buentjen, Principal Public Management Specialist, SDCC for their feedback on earlier versions of the report.

ABBREVIATIONS

BKN	Badan Kepegawaian Negara (National Civil Service Agency)
BOS	Bantuan Operasional Sekolah (Operational School Assistance Program)
InCiSE	International Civil Service Effectiveness Index
INDO-DAPOER	Indonesia Database for Policy and Economic Research
KPK	Komisi Pemberantasan Korupsi (Indonesian Anti-Corruption Commission)
LAN	Lembaga Administrasi Negara (National Institute of Public Administration)
MenPAN	Kementerian Pendayagunaan Aparatur Negara dan Reformasi Birokrasi (Ministry for Administration and Bureaucratic Reform)
OECD	Organisation for Economic Co-operation and Development
PNS	pegawai negeri sipil (permanent civil servants)
PPPK	pegawai pemerintah dengan perjanjian kerja (government employees with a work agreement)

1. INTRODUCTION

A modern civil service requires a skilled, competent, and adaptive workforce that is able to address increasingly complex policy challenges, navigate a demanding regulatory and legal environment, collaborate with a team in accomplishing tasks, engage with and deliver public services to a diverse citizenry, and improve government transparency and accountability. Civil servants not only need to be "qualified, impartial, values-driven, and ethical" (OECD 2017) but also able to deal with a rapidly evolving governance and technological environment. A modern civil service requires a comprehensive human resources management framework that prioritizes the development of talent to deliver "citizen-centric" services in the 21st century (OECD and ADB 2019).

This sector diagnostic study provides a broad, data-driven overview of the current state of Indonesia's civil service, including its basic organizational structure and state of its human resources. We examine in particular the competencies and skills of the public sector workforce, including Indonesia's education sector and the issues of gender and diversity and the institutional context and governance environment of the civil service. Finally, this report also considers the capacity of the Indonesian bureaucracy to effectively deliver services.

To provide a comprehensive picture of the current state of the Indonesian bureaucracy, the report draws on comprehensive data relating to individual civil servants of the National Civil Service Agency (BKN), data on service delivery from the World Bank's Indonesia Database for Policy and Economic Research (INDO-DAPOER),[1] public opinion surveys from the Asian Barometer,[2] and other aggregate data sources as well as secondary literature.

The report identifies several key issues:

1. The structure of the Indonesian civil service replicates many features of bureaucracies around the world in terms of its internal organization, size, pay structure, and basic rules of operation.

2. The national average indicators of the civil service's size and diversity and the competence and performance of civil servants mask a wide spatial variation across the country.

3. In skills and competency, Indonesian civil servants overall demonstrate lower than expected levels of educational attainment, which vary for the most part across the levels of government and across regional government units.

---

[1] Indonesia Database for Policy and Economic Research. https://datacatalog.worldbank.org/dataset/indonesia-database-policy-and-economic-research.

[2] Asian Barometer. http://www.asianbarometer.org/data/data-release.

4. It is unclear to what extent existing recruiting practices and on-the-job training programs address the current and future needs of Indonesia's civil service.
5. The example of Indonesia's education sector exemplifies many of the ongoing challenges to improved governance. Despite the well-intentioned reforms and an influx of fiscal resources into the education sector, Indonesian schools have not shown much improvement in the quality of service delivery.
6. Historically, gender diversity in the civil service has been weak.
7. Administrative data are collected and available, but these are not standardized and used adequately in policy-making decisions.
8. While a modernized regulatory framework, decentralization, and the creation of many new district governments have brought forth opportunities for change and improvements in service delivery, reforms have also created new challenges.

2. HUMAN RESOURCES IN INDONESIA'S CIVIL SERVICE

As of 2018, Indonesia's civil service employs about 4.2 million active civil servants, a decline from roughly 4.5 million in 2009 (Figure 2.1). The 2009–2018 decline is attributed to the growing waves of retirement, paired with the strict quota on the intake of new civil servants, and the 5-year moratorium on hiring announced by the Widodo government in 2014.[3] The civil service workforce currently makes up about 1.58% of the population, which is comparable to the size of bureaucracies in other countries in the region (Tjiptoherijanto 2007). As a share of total employment, the Indonesian public sector is below average compared with the Organisation for Economic Co-operation and Development (OECD) average and even the average among Southeast Asian nations (OECD and ADB 2019, p. 57). This workforce costs the state about 25% of its total revenue.

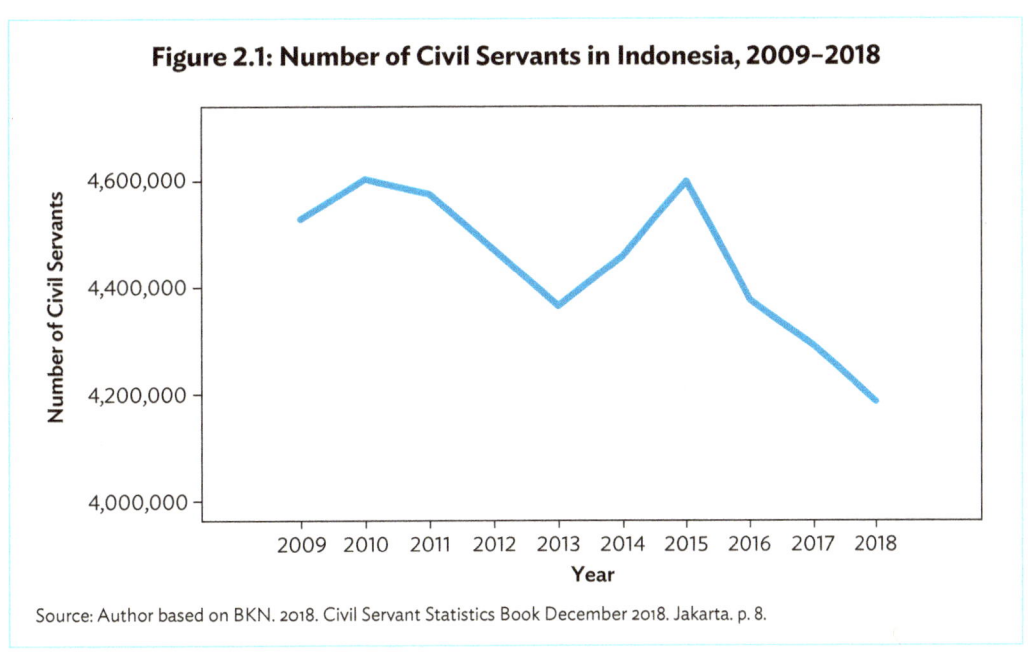

Figure 2.1: Number of Civil Servants in Indonesia, 2009–2018

Source: Author based on BKN. 2018. Civil Servant Statistics Book December 2018. Jakarta. p. 8.

---

[3] The temporary increase in the number of civil servants in 2015 was due to the change in retirement regulations, which extended the employment of civil servants originally scheduled to retire.

Civil servants are employed by more than 600 distinct national, regional, and local government units (32 ministries at the national level, 4 of which are coordinating ministries);[4] and several other agencies, bureaus, and organizations. Table 2.1 lists the top 10 national civil service organizations by number of employees as of 2015.

Table 2.1: Number of Employees in National Civil Service Units, 2015

Unit	No. of Employees
Kementerian Agama	232,700
Kementerian Riset, Teknologi, Dan Pendidikan Tinggi	112,777
Kementerian Keuangan	69,089
Kementerian Pertahanan	58,500
Kementerian Kesehatan	50,732
Kementerian Hukum Dan Hak Asasi Manusia	43,056
Mahkamah Agung RI	30,439
Kementerian Perhubungan	26,803
Kepolisian negara	24,381
Kementerian Pekerjaan Umum Dan Perumahan Rakyat	22,723

Source: Author.

Since the decentralization reforms in 1999 and 2004,[5] the Indonesian government has been organized in three layers—the central government, the *pemerintah provinsi* (provincial governments), and the *pemerintah kabupaten* and *kota* (district level governments). Indonesia's civil service is spread out across these government layers. Table 2.2 shows the distribution of civil servants between central and regional (provincial and district) governments. As of 2018, less than 1 million civil servants (22.44%) are employed in central government institutions, with the remaining 3.2 million in provincial and district governments.

Table 2.2: Number of Civil Servants by Level of Government, 2018

Type of Employee	Total	Percentage
Central government employees	939,236	22.44
Regional government employees	3,246,267	77.56

Source: Author.

Figure 2.2 shows the evolution of these divisions from 2009 to 2018, indicating a high level of stability in the share of central versus regional government employees.

Table 2.3 provides more detailed information on the total number of regional civil servants (district governments plus provincial governments) by province. Given their high levels of population density, it is not surprising that the provinces of Central Java, East Java, and West Java have the highest number of civil servants, with more than 300,000 employees in each province. In contrast, the provinces of West Sulawesi, North Kalimantan, and Bangka Belitung have the lowest number of civil servants.

---

[4] Coordinating Ministry for Political, Legal, and Security Affairs; Coordinating Ministry for Economic Affairs; Coordinating Ministry for Maritime Affairs and Investment; and Ministry for Human Development and Culture.

[5] Laws No. 22/1999, No. 25/1999, and No. 32/2004. Law No. 23/2014 clarified the earlier provisions.

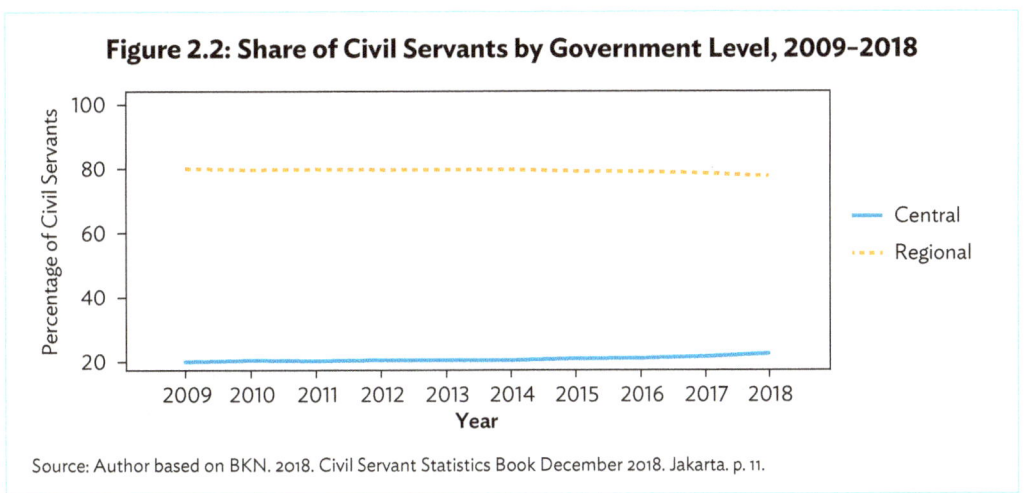

Figure 2.2: Share of Civil Servants by Government Level, 2009–2018

Source: Author based on BKN. 2018. Civil Servant Statistics Book December 2018. Jakarta. p. 11.

Table 2.3: Total Number of Civil Servants (Including District Employees) by Province, 2018

Province	No. of Employees
Pemerintah Aceh	131,521
Pemerintah Provinsi Sumatera Utara	192,135
Pemerintah Provinsi Riau	87,071
Pemerintah Provinsi Sumatera Barat	103,011
Pemerintah Provinsi Jambi	63,195
Pemerintah Provinsi Sumatera Selatan	109,511
Pemerintah Provinsi Kep. Bangka Belitung	26,156
Pemerintah Provinsi Bengkulu	48,670
Pemerintah Provinsi Lampung	99,711
Pemerintah Provinsi Daerah Khusus Ibukota Jakarta	66,225
Pemerintah Provinsi Jawa Barat	309,217
Pemerintah Provinsi Banten	73,367
Pemerintah Daerah D I Yogyakarta	48,179
Pemerintah Provinsi Jawa Tengah	325,256
Pemerintah Provinsi Jawa Timur	356,902
Pemerintah Provinsi Kalimantan Barat	74,416
Pemerintah Provinsi Kalimantan Tengah	62,644
Pemerintah Provinsi Kalimantan Selatan	70,612
Pemerintah Provinsi Kalimantan Timur	65,978
Pemerintah Provinsi Sulawesi Utara	57,312
Pemerintah Provinsi Gorontalo	28,037
Pemerintah Provinsi Sulawesi Tengah	75,875
Pemerintah Provinsi Sulawesi Selatan	157,422
Pemerintah Provinsi Sulawesi Tenggara	71,097
Pemerintah Provinsi Bali	66,548
Pemerintah Provinsi NTB	74,778
Pemerintah Provinsi NTT	105,514
Pemerintah Provinsi Maluku	53,845
Pemerintah Provinsi Maluku Utara	38,037
Pemerintah Provinsi Papua	89,342
Pemerintah Provinsi Kepulauan Riau	27,487
Pemerintah Provinsi Papua Barat	37,705
Pemerintah Provinsi Sulawesi Barat	3,064
Pemerintah Provinsi Kalimantan Utara	18,851
Total	**3,246,267**

Source: Author based on BKN. 2018. Civil Servant Statistics Book December 2018. Jakarta. p. 38.

Figure 2.3 depicts the geographic distribution of civil servants across Indonesian districts per 1,000 people. The map shows that the share of civil service employees (of the total local population) varies quite a bit across Indonesian geography. In the island of Papua, despite its overall low population density and low socioeconomic development, the size of the public sector, by number of civil servants, is much larger than in other parts of Indonesia. Similarly, parts of Kalimantan also have above average density in civil servants. In contrast, on the island of Java, where population density is unusually high, the civil service caters to a disproportionally large population. This indicates a possibly important dimension of spatial unevenness in the distribution of civil servants.

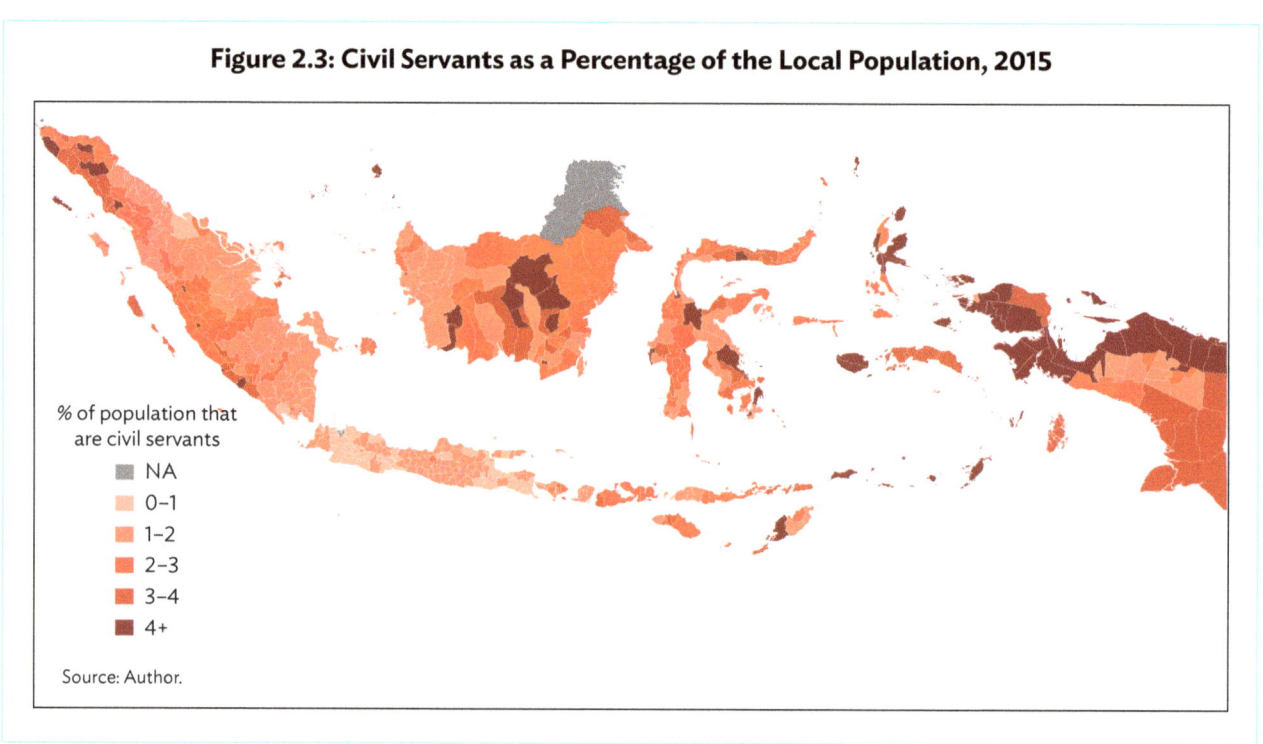

Figure 2.3: Civil Servants as a Percentage of the Local Population, 2015

Source: Author.

A similar pattern of spatial inequality emerges for specific job categories. Figure 2.4 shows the distribution of midwives (per 1,000 people) across districts in Indonesia, while Figure 2.5 presents the distribution of teachers (per 1,000 people). Teachers seem to be more evenly distributed across Indonesia, while specialized health care workers, such as midwives, display a large degree of spatial unevenness.

Internally, civil servants are classified into three broad categories: structural, functional–general, and functional–special. The latter two categories comprise the bulk of civil servants, including teachers, nurses, and agricultural extension workers (88.97% of all civil servants). Structural employees are hierarchically set above functional employees, typically with managerial responsibilities. Table 2.4 provides the number of employees in each category, with additional breakdown by gender. As discussed in more detail in section 3, men are overrepresented among structural employees, whereas women have roughly equal representation among functional employees.

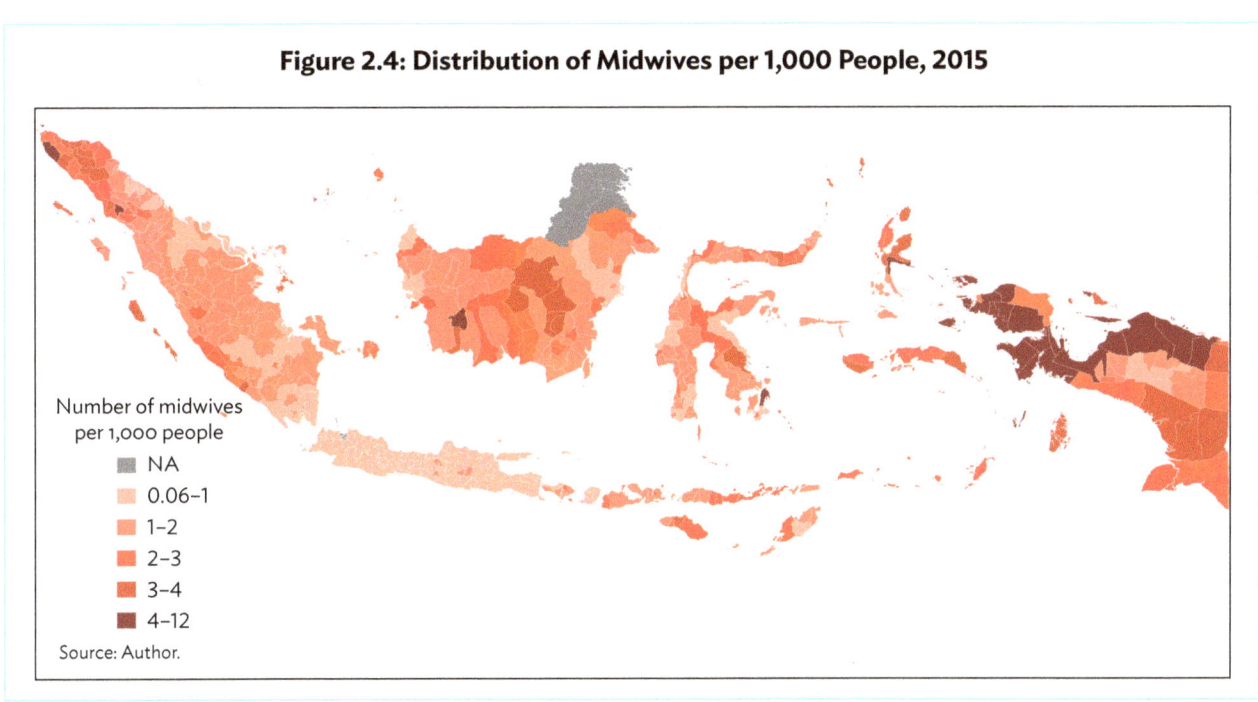

Figure 2.4: Distribution of Midwives per 1,000 People, 2015

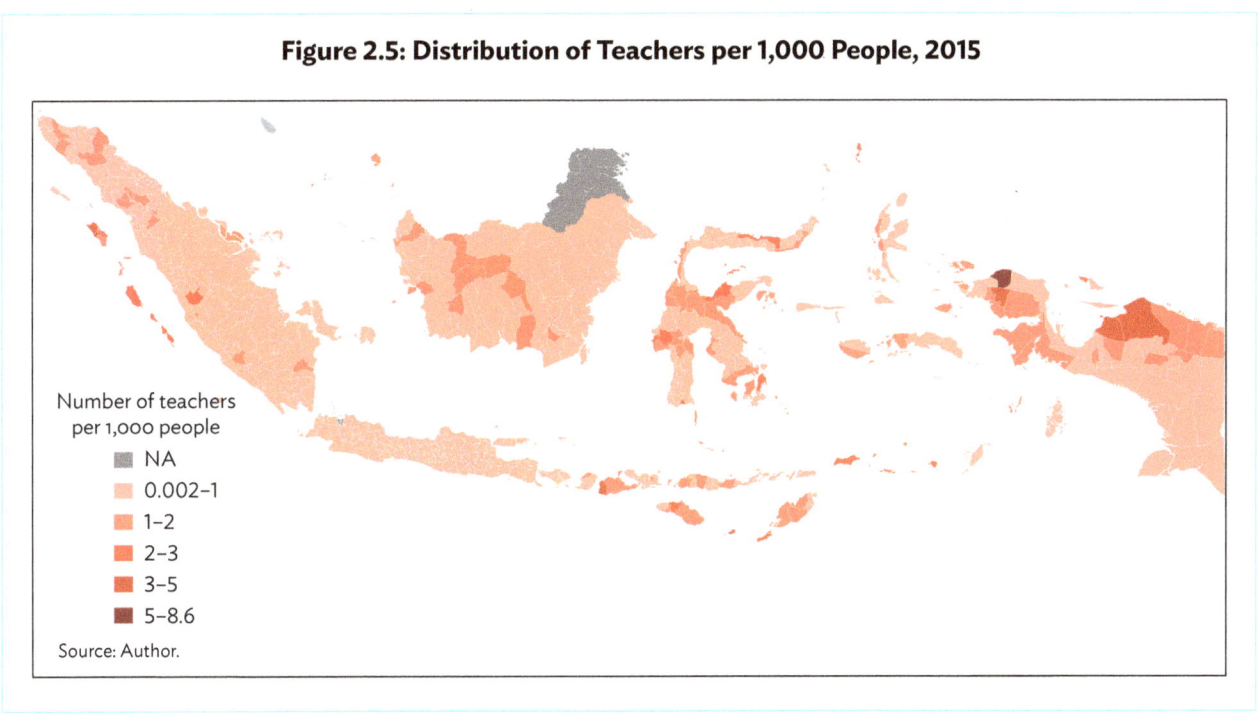

Figure 2.5: Distribution of Teachers per 1,000 People, 2015

Table 2.4: Number of Civil Servants by Type, 2015

Type	Men	%	Women	%	Total	%
Structural	309,624	7.40	151,862	3.63	461,486	11.03
Functional-Special	834,731	19.94	1,333,144	31.85	2,167,875	51.79
Functional-General	926,955	22.15	629,187	15.03	1,556,142	37.18
Total	**2,071,310**	**49.49**	**2,114,193**	**50.51**	**4,185,503**	**100**

Source: Author.

Figure 2.6 visualizes the overall breakdown across categories.

Figure 2.6: Share of Civil Servants by Type, 2018

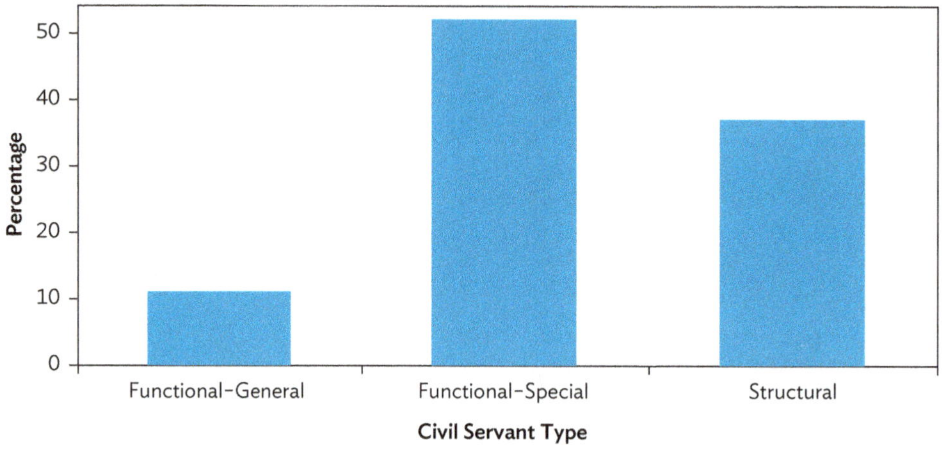

[Bar chart showing: Functional-General ~11%, Functional-Special ~52%, Structural ~37%]

Source: Author based on BKN. 2018. Civil Servant Statistics Book December 2018. Jakarta. p. 17.

In the category of functional civil servants with a special function, Figure 2.7 gives a breakdown by job type. Among the civil servants under this class, teachers are by far the most common type.

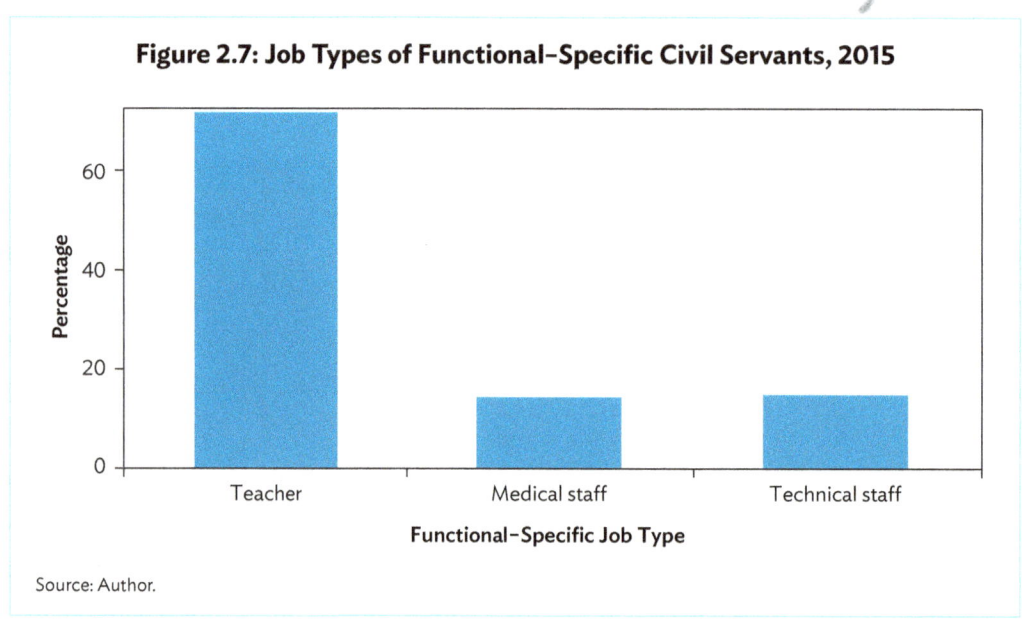

Figure 2.7: Job Types of Functional-Specific Civil Servants, 2015

Source: Author.

Overall, Indonesia's civil service shares many common structural features with civil service organizations around the world. The organizational division into (i) central government line ministries with functional specialization, (ii) a smaller number of cross-cutting coordinating ministries, and (iii) regional government units that partition the country into a set of governments with equal responsibilities, can be found in many other low-, middle-, and high-income countries. Similarly, the internal organization of the civil service along a strict hierarchy, with the vast majority of civil servants hired for specialized functions and a smaller cadre of core civil servants in leadership—can be found in many other settings.

In attempting to accommodate a highly diverse population spread across a large and heterogeneous geography, Indonesia's decentralized government structure generates a large degree of spatial unevenness in administrative penetration nationwide. As the figures above illustrate, Indonesia's civil service is spread unevenly across the country (in terms of the overall number of employees and specialized staff), generating particular challenges in its organization and management.

Indonesia's civil service also has a skewed age distribution. Table 2.5 provides a breakdown of civil servants across age brackets. Less than 20% of them are below the age of 35 and roughly 35% are aged 51 years and older. The distribution of men and women across age brackets is roughly similar (Figure 2.8). Given the age skew in the number of civil servants, careful retirement planning is necessary to avoid abrupt skill shortages across ministries and regional governments. A World Bank report (Sacks and Pierskalla 2018) indicates that about 22% of the current workforce will reach retirement age within the next 15 years. Expected retirement patterns also vary substantially across job types and the geography of district governments.

Table 2.5: Indonesian Civil Servants by Age Bracket and Gender, 2018

Age Bracket	Gender				Total	
	Men		Women			
18–20	5,513	0.13%	3,402	0.08%	8,915	0.21%
21–25	27,956	0.67%	17,009	0.41%	44,965	1.07%
26–30	62,782	1.50%	8,546	2.04%	148,242	3.54%
31–35	202,305	4.83%	299,889	7.16%	502,194	12.00%
36–40	298,174	7.12%	362,867	8.67%	661,041	15.79%
41–45	296,245	7.08%	303,819	7.26%	600,064	14.34%
46–50	389,189	9.30%	371,291	8.87%	76,048	18.17%
51–55	487,455	11.65%	415,523	9.93%	902,978	21.57%
56–60	292,133	6.98%	251,481	6.01%	543,614	12.99%
> 60	9,558	0.23%	3,452	0.08%	1,301	0.31%
Total	**2,071,310**	**49.49%**	**2,114,193**	**50.51%**	**4,185,503**	**100%**

Source: Author based on BKN. 2018. Civil Servant Statistics Book December 2018. Jakarta. p. 28.

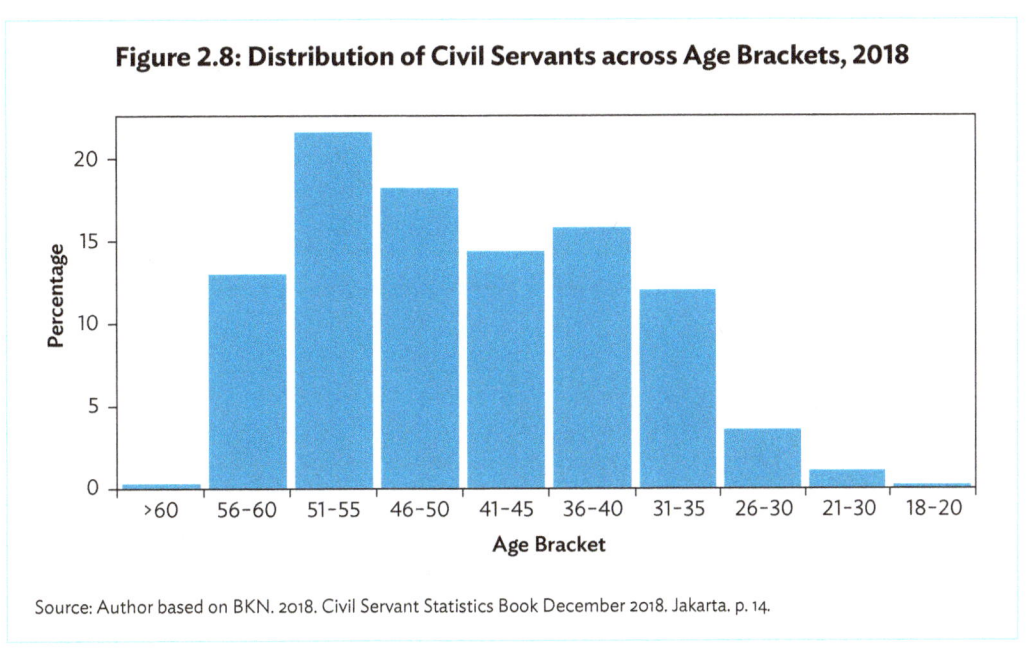

Figure 2.8: Distribution of Civil Servants across Age Brackets, 2018

Source: Author based on BKN. 2018. Civil Servant Statistics Book December 2018. Jakarta. p. 14.

3. CAPACITY AND SKILLS

Meritocratic principles are thought to be a crucial component of modern and effective bureaucracies, with important implications for the delivery of public services, growth, and improvement in human welfare (Pepinsky, Perskalla, and Sacks 2017; Evans and Rauch 1999). While there is broad consensus on the core features of an effective civil service—which include formalized entrance exams, secure tenure, the importance of meritocratic recruitment and promotion, and the non-politicization of jobs—bureaucracies in many countries fall short of that ideal (Rauch and Evans 2000).

One element of a meritocratic civil service is the selection and promotion of competent and skilled civil servants. As opposed to selecting civil servants based on personal loyalty or political calculations, meritocratic selection relies on the impartial assessment and rewarding of performance on the job. Civil servants need to be "qualified, impartial, values-driven and ethical" (OECD 2017), but increasingly complex governance challenges and a changing technological environment also press civil service organizations to recruit and develop specialized skills in the civil service workforce (OECD 2017). Modern civil service organizations have to tailor their skills needs based on specific tasks. For example, generating policy advice, interacting with clients, managing third-party providers, and overseeing projects across different units and jurisdictions all require different skill sets (OECD 2017).

While not a perfect proxy for a civil servant's quality, skill, or ability, a large literature on human capital in economics has identified educational attainment as a useful proxy. Since educational attainment predicts earnings, it proxies for skill—or at least the ability to *signal* one's skill level (Card 1999). Educational attainment has also been widely used in the study of political selection and the quality of political candidates (Besley and Reynal-Querol 2011; Ferraz and Finan 2009). For example, the massive expansion of schooling in Indonesia in the 1970s was found to have increased both the educational attainment of candidates for public office and the quality of associated public goods provision (Martinez-Bravo 2017). Empirical work on the bureaucracy of the People's Republic of China has also found that educated civil servants perform better at poverty alleviation (He and Wang 2017).[5]

Educational attainment among Indonesian civil servants varies widely. Figure 3.1 shows the distribution of civil servants by educational levels. As of 2018, the civil service had employees who had completed elementary school education (SD) as well as those with graduate-level university degrees (S2/S3). More than 50% of civil servants have a finished a 4-year university degree but a surprisingly large number of civil servants (20.59%)

---

[5] Selecting civil servants with a high degree of educational attainment or best on-the-job performance does not automatically imply a reduction of corruption or patronage in the civil service. For example, a recent study of civil servants in the health sector indicates that individuals paying the largest bribes to acquire a civil servant position also ended up being the most capable (Weaver 2020).

completed only high-school education. Table 3.1 shows a breakdown of overall educational attainment and gender.

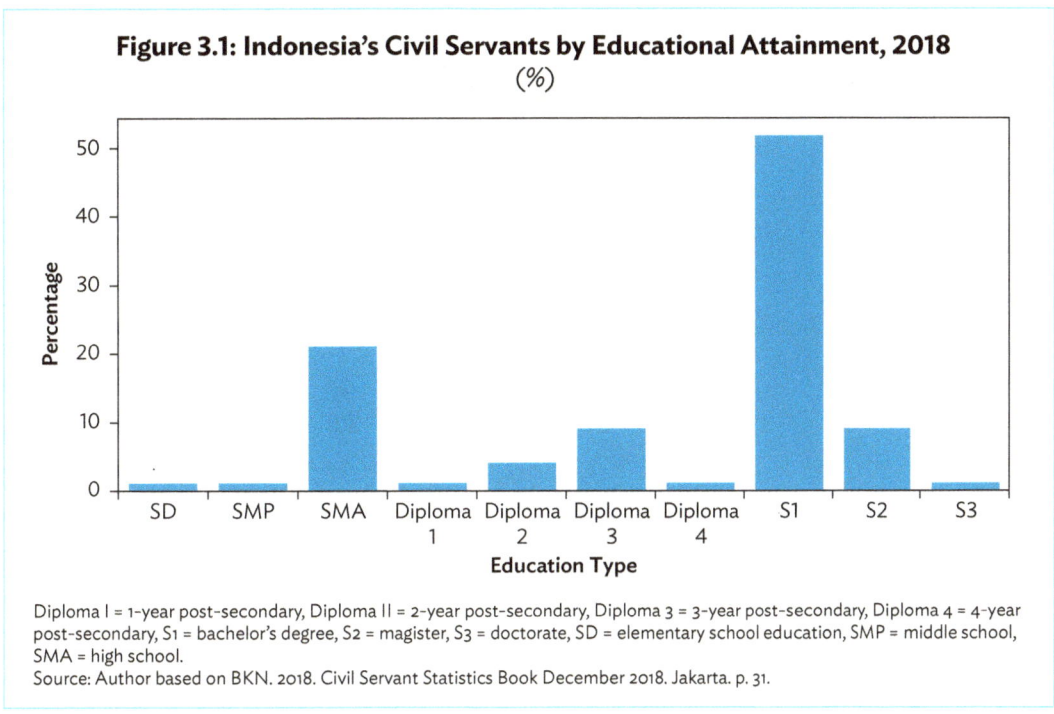

Figure 3.1: Indonesia's Civil Servants by Educational Attainment, 2018 (%)

Diploma I = 1-year post-secondary, Diploma II = 2-year post-secondary, Diploma 3 = 3-year post-secondary, Diploma 4 = 4-year post-secondary, S1 = bachelor's degree, S2 = magister, S3 = doctorate, SD = elementary school education, SMP = middle school, SMA = high school.
Source: Author based on BKN. 2018. Civil Servant Statistics Book December 2018. Jakarta. p. 31.

Table 3.1: Educational Attainment of Civil Servants by Gender, 2018

Education	Men	%	Women	%	Total	%
SD	27,626	0.66	2,237	0.05	29,863	0.71
SMP	47,633	1.14	6,157	0.15	53,790	1.29
SMA	545,288	13.03	316,713	7.57	862,001	20.59
Diploma I	22,193	0.53	20,422	0.49	42,615	1.02
Diploma II	71,005	1.70	10,365	2.48	174,655	4.17
Diploma III	117,496	2.81	274,106	6.55	391,602	9.36
Diploma IV	27,625	0.66	28,539	0.68	56,164	1.34
S1	973,593	23.26	1,201,733	28.71	2,175,326	51.97
S2	223,797	5.35	154,419	3.69	378,216	9.04
S3	15,054	0.36	6,217	0.15	21,271	0.51
Total	2,071,310	49.49	2,114,193	50.51	4,185,503	100

Diploma I = 1-year post-secondary, Diploma II = 2-year post-secondary, Diploma 3 = 3-year post-secondary, Diploma 4 = 4-year post-secondary, S1 = bachelor's degree, S2 = magister, S3 = doctorate, SD = elementary school education, SMP = middle school, SMA = high school.
Source: Author based on BKN. 2018. Civil Servant Statistics Book December 2018. Jakarta. p. 31.

More than 75% of all civil servants have some type of college education, 51.97% completed a 4-year bachelor's degree, but only 9.55% have attained post-graduate education. Male civil servants are overrepresented in the low educational attainment categories. Of those who had a high-school educational attainment or lower, roughly two-thirds are male and only one-third is female. Female civil servants are more likely to have completed a 4-year degree but are somewhat underrepresented among civil servants with post-graduate degree work. Table 3.2 provides further information on civil servants' educational attainment by age bracket.

Table 3.2: Educational Attainment of Civil Servants by Age Bracket, 2018

Age Bracket	SD	SLTP	SLTA	D-I	D-II	D-III	D-IV	S 1	S 2	S 3	Total
18–20	0	0	3,500	5,280	2	127	5	1	0	0	8,915
21–25	0	0	10,685	9,404	82	9,942	7,705	6,958	189	0	44,965
26–30	0	0	17,346	2,553	1,384	52,330	8,662	58,394	7,558	15	148,242
31–35	997	4,241	73,715	4,408	13,225	100,148	9,918	259,409	35,860	273	502,194
36–40	2,287	6,104	122,270	3,584	14,358	84,783	8,267	358,670	59,479	1,239	661,041
41–45	3,851	8,029	117,393	4,545	9,469	56,145	9,038	320,043	68,854	2,697	600,064
46–50	5,673	11,984	168,689	2,732	17,042	34,412	6,836	431,164	77,762	4,186	760,480
51–55	9,835	15,179	232,671	4,392	51,696	33,991	4,280	469,736	76,422	4,776	902,978
56–60	7,220	8,253	115,732	5,717	67,397	19,724	1,453	26,814	45,013	4,965	543,614
>60	0	0	0	0	0	0	0	2,811	7,079	3,120	13,010
Total	**29,863**	**53,790**	**862,001**	**42,615**	**174,655**	**391,602**	**56,164**	**2,175,326**	**378,216**	**21,271**	**4,185,503**

Diploma I = 1-year post-secondary, Diploma II = 2-year post-secondary, Diploma 3 = 3-year post-secondary, Diploma 4 = 4-year post-secondary, S1 = bachelor's degree, S2 = magister, S3 = doctorate, SD = elementary school education, SLTP = junior high school, SLTA = senior high school.
Source: Author based on BKN. 2018. Civil Servant Statistics Book December 2018. Jakarta. p. 30.

Table 3.3 gives a summary of educational attainment across echelon levels and disaggregated by gender. To calculate the educational attainment for each group, we assigned the codes 1 = SD; 2 = SMP; 3 = SMA; 4 = Diploma 1–3; 5 = Diploma 4/S1; and 6 = S2/S3. The average educational attainment for functional employees below the echelon is at 4.38 and 4.09 for women and men, respectively, lower than in any echelon level. In the higher echelon levels, the average educational attainment increases for both men and women. Female educational attainment is higher, on average, only among functional civil servants and lower or equivalent for all other categories. In the top echelon 1 level, average educational attainment is 5.24 for women and 5.5 for men. These summary statistics indicate a substantial variation in the degree of educational attainment across the echelon hierarchy.

Table 3.3: Education of All Civil Servants by Gender and Echelon Level, 2015

Echelon Level	Gender	Average Education Level
Echelon 1	F	5.24
Echelon 1	M	5.50
Echelon 2	F	5.22
Echelon 2	M	5.39
Echelon 3	F	5.19
Echelon 3	M	5.19
Echelon 4	F	4.81
Echelon 4	M	4.83
Echelon 5	F	4.45
Echelon 5	M	4.50
Functional	F	4.38
Functional	M	4.09

F = female, M = male.
Source: Author.

Table 3.4 shows the same summary of educational attainment for civil servants, but only for those employed by the central government. Again, we find that average educational attainment increases across the echelon hierarchy. As before, female educational attainment is, on average, strictly higher only among functional employees and similar overall to the entire population of civil servants. Overall, average educational attainment is typically higher for central government employees across all echelon levels.

Table 3.4: Education Level of Central Government Civil Servants by Echelon and Gender, 2015

Echelon Level	Gender	Average Education
Echelon 1	F	5.2
Echelon 1	M	5.5
Echelon 2	F	5.5
Echelon 2	M	5.5
Echelon 3	F	5.2
Echelon 3	M	5.3
Echelon 4	F	5.0
Echelon 4	M	5.2
Echelon 5	F	4.6
Echelon 5	M	4.6
Functional	F	4.6
Functional	M	4.3

F = female, M = male.
Source: Author.

Table 3.5 displays the same breakdown for regional (provincial and district government) employees who, on average, have lower educational attainment across the echelon hierarchy. In gender disparities, female civil servants at the regional level have higher educational attainment at echelon levels 5 and 4 but show disproportionately lower levels of educational attainment compared with central civil servants at echelon level 2.

Table 3.5: Educational Level of Regional Civil Servants by Echelon and Gender, 2015

Echelon Level	Gender	Average Education
Echelon 1	F	5.27
Echelon 1	M	5.58
Echelon 2	F	5.12
Echelon 2	M	5.36
Echelon 3	F	5.17
Echelon 3	M	5.18
Echelon 4	F	4.78
Echelon 4	M	4.76
Echelon 5	F	4.23
Echelon 5	M	4.21
Functional	F	4.34
Functional	M	4.02

F = female, M = male.
Source: Author.

Table 3.6 depicts average educational attainment across the echelon hierarchy, separated by central versus regional employees, but disregarding any gender differences. Except for echelon 1, central government employees have a higher average educational attainment. The discrepancy is largest at echelon 4, with central employees having average educational attainment scores of 5.1, whereas regional employees only report 4.77, a difference of 0.33 points.

Table 3.6: Average Educational Attainment by Echelon and Government Levels, 2015

Echelon Level	Government Level	Average Education Attainment
Echelon 1	Regional	5.51
Echelon 1	Central	5.43
Echelon 2	Regional	5.32
Echelon 2	Central	5.54
Echelon 3	Regional	5.18
Echelon 3	Central	5.25
Echelon 4	Regional	4.77
Echelon 4	Central	5.10
Echelon 5	Regional	4.22
Echelon 5	Central	4.60
Functional	Regional	4.19
Functional	Central	4.40

Source: Author.

Differences in educational attainment are more pronounced when comparing central government departments. Table 3.7 lists the 20 largest national civil service units by educational attainment. Across these units, average educational attainment varies from 2.98 to 5.36. The top national units include the Audit Board of the Republic of Indonesia; the Ministry for Research, Technology, and Higher Education; and the Ministry of Home Affairs. The national units with the lowest average educational attainment among large departments are the State Police (civilian administrators only), the Ministry of Defense (civilian administrators only), and the Ministry of Transportation. The table indicates that departments dealing with more complex technical topics tend to attract and recruit highly educated civil servants.

Table 3.7: Largest National Departments and Agencies by Education Level, 2015

Department	Average Education Level
Audit Board of the Republic of Indonesia	5.36
Ministry of Research, Technology and Higher Education	5.19
Ministry of Home Affairs	4.97
Supreme Court of the Republic of Indonesia	4.47
Ministry of Finance	4.45
Ministry of Health	4.37
Ministry of Religious Affairs	4.33
Ministry of Education and Culture	4.23
Ministry of Marine Affairs and Fisheries	4.21
Ministry of Agriculture	3.97
Attorney General's Office	3.87
Central Bureau of Statistics	3.75
Ministry of Public Works and Housing	3.74
Ministry of Environment and Forestry	3.66
Ministry of Communication and Information Technology	3.49
Ministry of Agrarian Affairs and Spatial Planning	3.45
Ministry of Law and Human Rights	3.45
Ministry of Transportation	3.44
State Police	4.00
Ministry of Defense	2.98

Source: Author.

Table 3.8 reports on average educational attainment for provincial governments. Average education ranges from only 4.17 in Papua, to a maximum of 4.9 in Banten. This indicates substantial spatial variation in the competence of civil servants, where poorer and more remote provincial governments rely on a less-educated workforce.

Table 3.8: Average Education Level of Civil Servants by Province, 2015

Province	Average Education Level
Pemerintah Provinsi Banten	4.90
Pemerintah Provinsi Sumatera Selatan	4.77
Pemerintah Provinsi Papua Barat	4.73
Pemerintah Provinsi Kepulauan Riau	4.72
Pemerintah Provinsi Sulawesi Selatan	4.71
Pemerintah Provinsi Bengkulu	4.71
Pemerintah Aceh	4.69
Pemerintah Provinsi Gorontalo	4.67
Pemerintah Provinsi Kep. Bangka Belitung	4.67
Pemerintah Provinsi Jawa Barat	4.66
Pemerintah Provinsi Kalimantan Utara	4.64
Pemerintah Provinsi Sulawesi Tenggara	4.59
Pemerintah Provinsi Sumatera Barat	4.58
Pemerintah Provinsi Jawa Tengah	4.58
Pemerintah Provinsi Bali	4.58
Pemerintah Provinsi Sumatera Utara	4.57
Pemerintah Provinsi Sulawesi Barat	4.57
Pemerintah Provinsi Kalimantan Tengah	4.56
Pemerintah Provinsi Sulawesi Utara	4.56
Pemerintah Provinsi Maluku Utara	4.55
Pemerintah Provinsi Riau	4.55
Pemerintah Provinsi Jambi	4.54
Pemerintah Provinsi Jawa Timur	4.53
Pemerintah Provinsi Lampung	4.53
Pemerintah Provinsi Ntt	4.50
Pemerintah Provinsi Sulawesi Tengah	4.46
Pemerintah Daerah D I Yogyakarta	4.45
Pemerintah Provinsi Maluku	4.44
Pemerintah Provinsi Ntb	4.43
Pemerintah Provinsi Kalimantan Barat	4.43
Pemerintah Provinsi Kalimantan Selatan	4.43
Pemerintah Provinsi Kalimantan Timur	4.42
Pemerintah Provinsi Daerah Khusus Ibukota Jakarta	4.23
Pemerintah Provinsi Papua	4.17

Source: Author.

Tables 3.9 and 3.10 indicate the average educational attainment for the top 10 and bottom 10 district governments. The overall range is even wider than for provincial governments, ranging from 3.54 in Kabupaten Malaka to 4.74 in Kota Serang. Among the top districts, localities close to Jakarta and those in Java are overrepresented. At the other end, the governments in Papua had the lowest educational attainment.

Table 3.9: Top-10 District Governments by Average Education Level, 2015

District	Average Education Level
Pemerintah Kota Serang	4.74
Pemerintah Kab. Pegunungan Arfak	4.70
Pemerintah Kota Cilegon	4.69
Pemerintah Kota Prabumulih	4.63
Pemerintah Kota Tangerang Selatan	4.62
Pemerintah Kab. Kepahiang	4.60
Pemerintah Kab. Sinjai	4.59
Pemerintah Kab. Sidenreng Rappang	4.58
Pemerintah Kab. Wajo	4.57
Pemerintah Kab. Blitar	4.57

Source: Author.

Table 3.10: Bottom-10 District Governments by Average Education Level, 2015

District	Average Education Level
Pemerintah Kab. Maluku Barat Daya	3.75
Pemerintah Kab. Dogiyai	3.74
Pemerintah Kab. Mappi	3.68
Pemerintah Kab. Alor	3.67
Pemerintah Kab. Jayawijaya	3.66
Pemerintah Kab. Timor Tengah Selatan	3.64
Pemerintah Kab. Belu	3.62
Pemerintah Kab. Tolikara	3.61
Pemerintah Kab. Puncak	3.58
Pemerintah Kab. Malaka	3.54

Source: Author.

Figure 3.2 visualizes the spatial distribution of average educational attainment across district governments. Papua is one of the regions with the lowest educational attainment of civil servants, whereas parts of Eastern and Western Java as well as parts of Kalimantan and Sumatra have the highest attainment.

The spatial difference in educational attainment is even more stark for specific technical job categories. For example, in Figure 3.3 the spatial distribution of average educational attainment of functional staff in the medical services area shows the region of Papua extremely lacking in skilled civil servants. In contrast, Eastern Java, parts of Sumatra, and Northern and Eastern Kalimantan have the highest educational attainment among their medical staff.

For teachers in the civil service a similar picture emerges. Teachers are the most common type of civil servant. While the overall spatial distribution of educational attainment displayed in Figure 3.4 is less extreme than for medical staff, it is important to note that the range of educational attainment of teachers as a job category is inherently smaller. Teachers in Sumatra, Sulawesi, parts of Papua, and Nusa Tenggara Timur have a particularly low level of educational attainment. Interestingly, there is substantial variation among district governments within Papua.

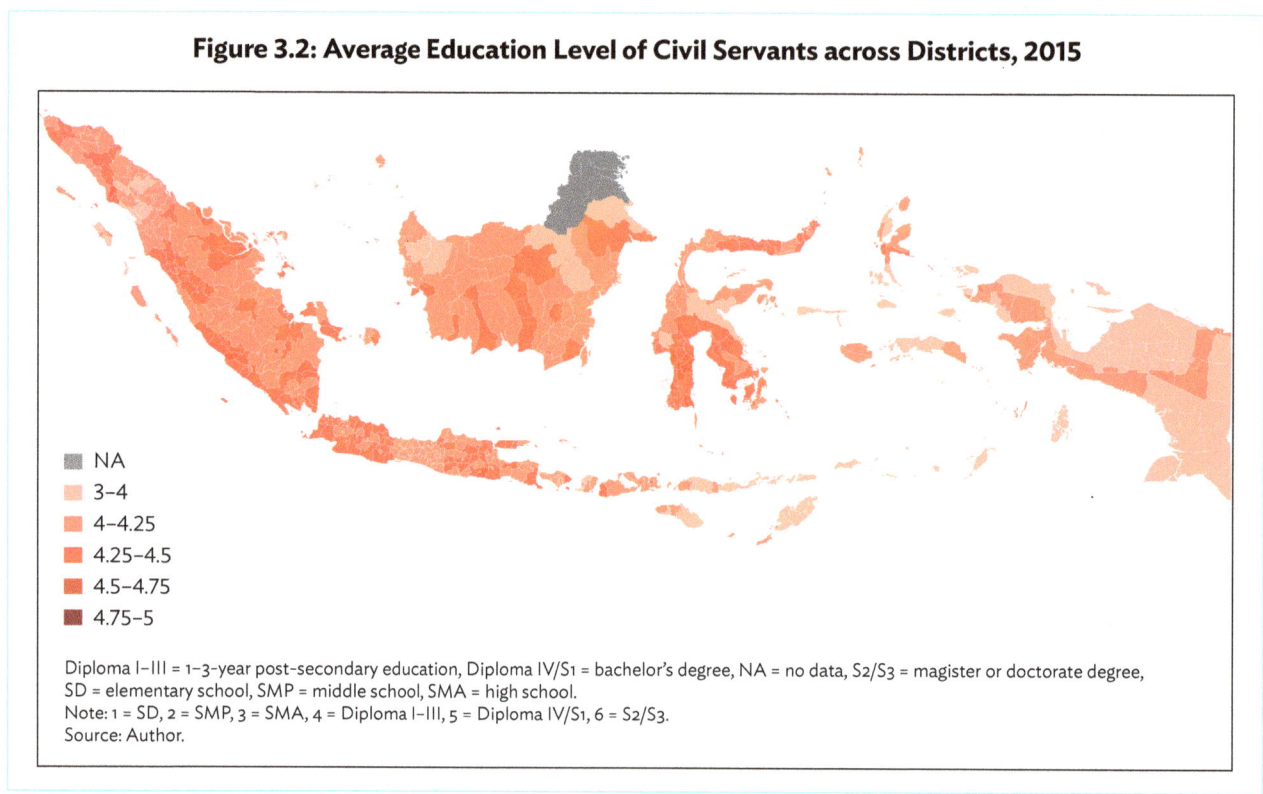

Figure 3.2: Average Education Level of Civil Servants across Districts, 2015

Diploma I–III = 1–3-year post-secondary education, Diploma IV/S1 = bachelor's degree, NA = no data, S2/S3 = magister or doctorate degree, SD = elementary school, SMP = middle school, SMA = high school.
Note: 1 = SD, 2 = SMP, 3 = SMA, 4 = Diploma I–III, 5 = Diploma IV/S1, 6 = S2/S3.
Source: Author.

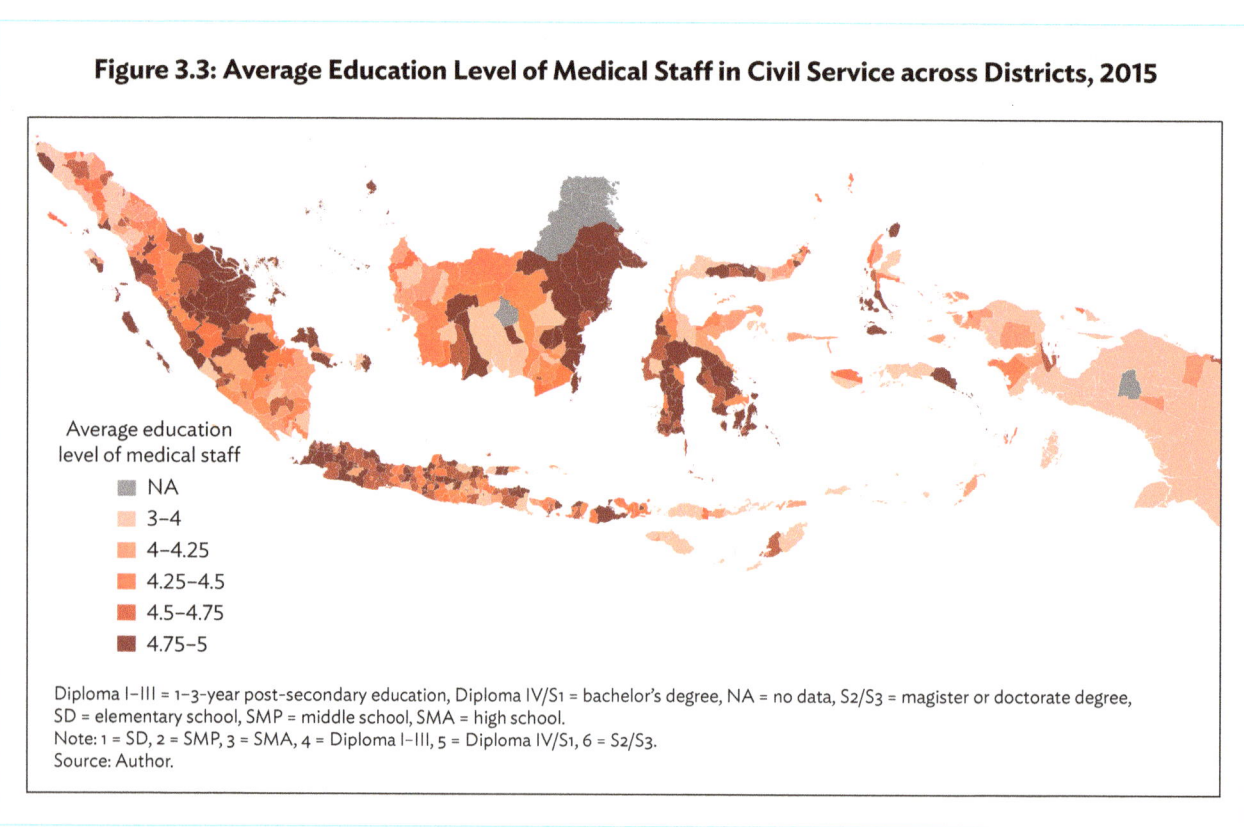

Figure 3.3: Average Education Level of Medical Staff in Civil Service across Districts, 2015

Diploma I–III = 1–3-year post-secondary education, Diploma IV/S1 = bachelor's degree, NA = no data, S2/S3 = magister or doctorate degree, SD = elementary school, SMP = middle school, SMA = high school.
Note: 1 = SD, 2 = SMP, 3 = SMA, 4 = Diploma I–III, 5 = Diploma IV/S1, 6 = S2/S3.
Source: Author.

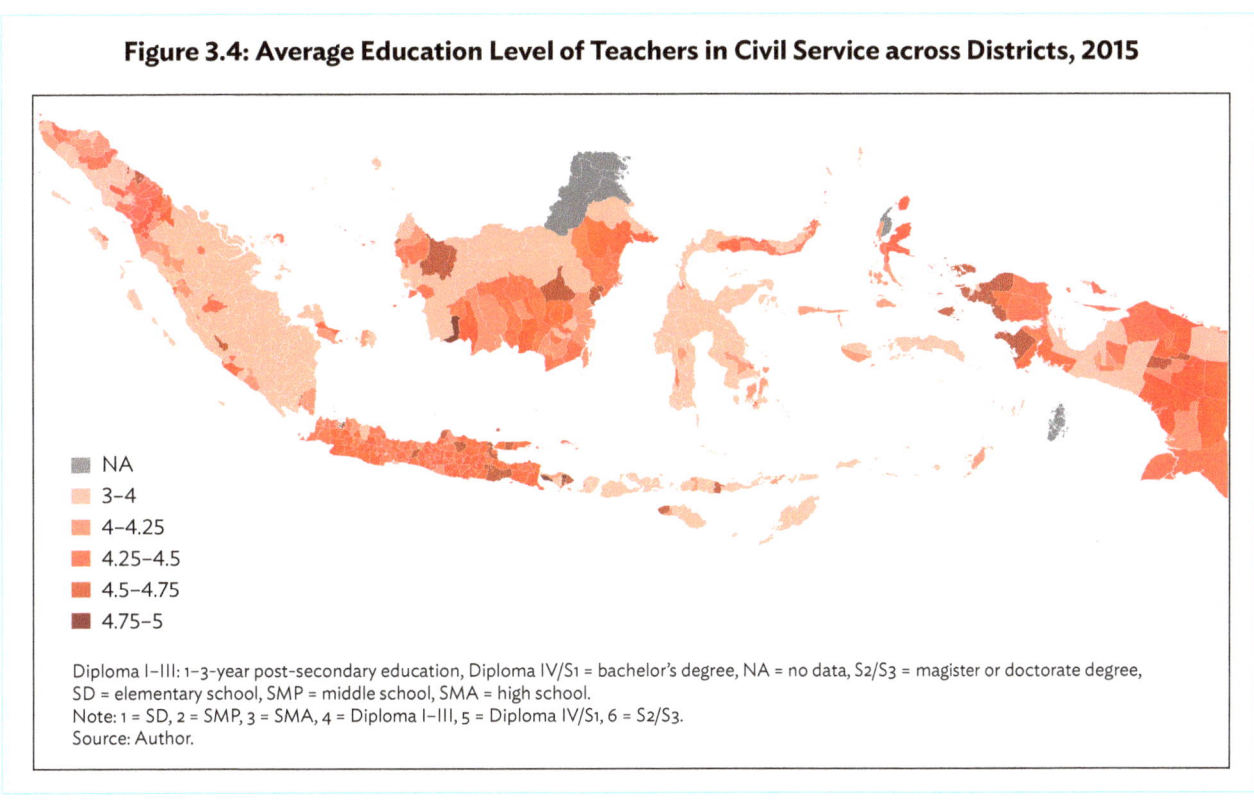

Figure 3.4: Average Education Level of Teachers in Civil Service across Districts, 2015

Diploma I–III: 1–3-year post-secondary education, Diploma IV/S1 = bachelor's degree, NA = no data, S2/S3 = magister or doctorate degree, SD = elementary school, SMP = middle school, SMA = high school.
Note: 1 = SD, 2 = SMP, 3 = SMA, 4 = Diploma I–III, 5 = Diploma IV/S1, 6 = S2/S3.
Source: Author.

Overall, the educational attainment of Indonesia's civil service varies substantially across its hierarchy, and throughout the national-level departments and agencies, space, and job type. The spatial inequality in skilled civil servants is particularly noteworthy and suggests an important issue to be addressed for the long-term management of the civil service.

Beyond the standard educational attainment, the Indonesian civil service also offers (and requires) additional training programs for civil servants (Tjiptoherijanto 2018). All civil servants are supposed to undergo a preservice training during their 1-year probationary period. In 2016, the National Institute of Public Administration (LAN) updated the basic design of the preservice training. The new preservice training (Diklat Prajabatan) is expected to last 3 months and cover basic information on the Indonesian civil service and review and habituate key values and goals of the civil service. Each ministry is also expected to add a component on technical proficiency, based on the civil servant's subject area. For structural employees, LAN offers a series of management training programs (Diklatpim I, II, III, and IV) such as training in management styles, effective communication, and the development of a policy brief. The National Leadership Training (Diklat PIMTI) is a new training course designed for echelon 1 civil servants to increase their understanding of government policies and the policy-making process, while the Reform Leaders Academy Training draws leaders of local and central government units at echelon levels 1 and 2 for a specialized 16-week, on- and off-campus training course, which culminates in the production of a joint policy paper. For functional employees, workshops for general competence (*diklat fungsional keahlian*) and specific skills (*diklat fungsional ketrampilan*) are typically organized through LAN. Similarly, structural and functional employees have access to technical training offered by their specific government institution (*diklat teknis substantif*) or general technical training (*diklat teknis umum*), such as for project management skills, at LAN. LAN also offers a 5-day "Mental Revolution Training," which focuses on changing civil servants' mindset toward making the civil service more productive and responsive to the welfare needs of Indonesian citizens.

Individual civil servants also have access to external educational opportunities. Most prominently, the national LPDP Scholarship Program allows civil servants access to limited funding for additional educational certification. The LPDP program provides financial support for Indonesian citizens who wish to pursue degree programs in Indonesia and abroad. In 2018, 1,789 individuals (964 domestic, 825 overseas) received a scholarship for master and doctoral programs. A small fraction of those scholarships was awarded to civil servants who were pursuing additional degree training.

Indonesia's civil service has a developed infrastructure for skill development and training via the National Civil Service Agency (BKN) and the National Institute for Administration, including the various local and national training centers, training centers in various ministries, and the Schools of Administrative Science in Jakarta, Bandung, and Makassar (Politeknik STIA LAN). As of 2016, LAN oversees 52 accredited training institutions. LAN is also developing e-training capabilities for the various training programs. Any efforts to improve the training of civil servants will have to build on this existing infrastructure.

Despite the established infrastructure for training and development, there has yet to be conducted a rigorous and comprehensive evaluation, via a randomized-controlled trial, of the effectiveness of these training programs, for example. To what extent these training programs have causally improved the knowledge, skills, and job performance of civil servants is unknown. Moreover, not all civil service organizations have been able to complete the numerical targets of civil service training for the different employee categories (see for example the LAN Annual Report 2018 or the Professionalism Index Assessment mentioned below).

It is also unclear if the existing framework fully satisfies the current or future needs of civil service units. Ministry Regulation RB No. 38 promulgated in 2017 required all civil service organizations to develop competency standards, meant to modernize the recruitment and talent development of the civil service, but few units have completed this task—2018 data from the Ministry for Administrative and Bureaucratic Reform (MenPAN) revealed that across central agencies, provincial governments, and district governments, only few had implemented comprehensive competency standards (Suwitri et al. 2019)

Consider, for example, the key issue of digital competency in Indonesia's civil service, an area of crucial importance going forward. Public service delivery increasingly relies on complex information technology infrastructure to deliver services and organize key organizational processes (e.g., e-government services and e-procurement). Civil servants need to acquire and maintain the necessary skills for operating e-government services. Relatedly, civil servants need to be trained in practices of data security and privacy to safeguard sensitive government information. Communication and outreach by government service providers to citizens must also increasingly make use of social media, therefore civil servants must train in the appropriate use of social media platforms. Given these demands, it is revealing that a review of public sector practices by the OECD and the Asian Development Bank (ADB) (2019) records that the Indonesian government does not mention digital competency in its civil service competency framework (Figure 3.5).

In addition to a coarse metric like educational attainment, Indonesia's civil service uses additional metrics to assess performance. In particular, BKN developed a new Professionalism Index, which was mandated by Law 5/2014 and Presidential Regulation 11/2017 and further specified in the Ministry of the State Apparatus' Permenpan RB No. 38 in 2018, with implementation guidelines spelled out in BKN Regulation No. 8 in 2019. The index provides a holistic assessment of a civil service unit's professionalism, based on four components: qualification, competence, discipline, and performance. The qualification of a civil servant is measured by educational attainment (weighted at 25% of the final score), competence is assessed by completion of additional training workshops (weighted at 40% of the final score), performance is based on annual performance assessments (weighted at 30%), and discipline by records of disciplinary infractions (weighted at 5%). The final score ranges from "very low" (<60), "low" (61–70), "moderate" (71–80), "high" (81–90), to

Figure 3.5: Digital Competency of Governments, 2019

	Digital competencies mentioned in competency frameworks	Employee development is a key competency for SCS
Brunei Darussalam	○	○
Cambodia	○	○
Indonesia	○	○
Lao PDR	○	○
Malaysia	○	●
Philippines	○	●
Singapore	○	●
Thailand	●	●
Viet Nam	●	○
SEA Total	**2**	**4**
Australia	○	○
Republic of Korea	○	○
Japan	○	○
New Zealand	…	●
OECD Total	**13**	**11**

● Yes ○ No

ADB = Asian Development Bank, Lao PDR = Lao People's Democratic Republic, OECD = Organisation for Economic Co-operation and Development, SCS = senior civil service, SEA = Southeast Asia.
Source: OECD and ADB. 2019. *Government at a Glance Southeast Asia 2019*. Paris: OECD Publishing. p. 32.

"very high" (91–100). This index relies on a reasonable set of input metrics that reflect standard expectations for professional civil service. Since no details on reliability and validation exercises are reported by BKN, the extent to which this measurement approach is valid and reliable remains unclear.

To collect data for the initial Professionalism Index, BKN surveyed about 1.5 million civil servants (36.6% of all civil servants). The response rates varied greatly across civil service units. BKN did not seem to have followed a random-sampling procedure in data collection but relied instead on self-reporting by civil service units. This means that despite the large number of responses, there is no assurance that the Professionalism Index score is representative of the Indonesian civil service as a whole (or for specific organizations) because reporting is most likely correlated with underlying levels of professionalism.

Despite these caveats, the Professionalism Index reveals an interesting pattern. Table 3.11 lists the Professionalism Index scores for various civil service organizations. Overall, central government units scored an average of 68.5 (out of 100), and regional government units scored 62.7, indicating "low" professionalism across the board according to BKN classification.

Figure 3.6 presents the distribution of Professionalism Index scores for Indonesian district governments. Two things are of note. First, district governments overall have a lower professionalism score than central government units. Second, as with many other civil service indicators, there is substantial geographic variation across districts.

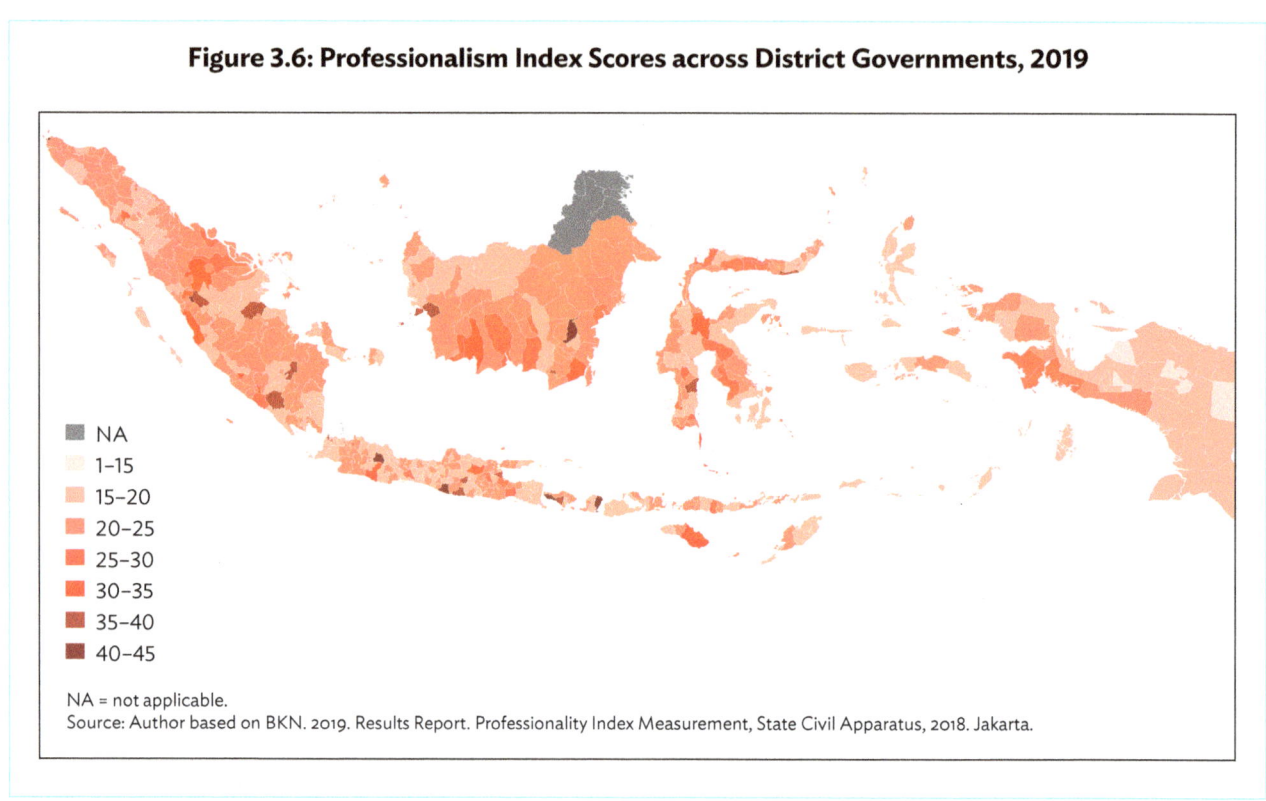

Figure 3.6: Professionalism Index Scores across District Governments, 2019

NA = not applicable.
Source: Author based on BKN. 2019. Results Report. Professionality Index Measurement, State Civil Apparatus, 2018. Jakarta.

Table 3.11: Performance of Civil Servants in Indonesia, 2018

Agency	Percentage of Respondents (%)	Dimension				IP Value	Category
		Qualification	Competence	Performance	Discipline		
Central agencies	**34.90**	**14.70**	**24.00**	**24.80**	**5.00**	**68.50**	**Low**
Ministries	38.20	14.20	23.20	24.30	5.00	66.70	Low
Institutes	19.60	15.10	24.70	25.40	5.00	72.50	Moderate
Regional agencies	**37.10**	**13.40**	**20.70**	**23.50**	**5.00**	**62.70**	**Low**
Provincial governments	39.60	14.20	21.70	24.20	5.00	65.10	Low
District governments	36.50	12.70	19.80	22.90	5.00	60.30	Low
All	**36.60**	**14.10**	**22.40**	**24.20**	**5.00**	**65.90**	**Low**

IP = Indeks Profesional/Professionalism Index.
Source: Author based on BKN. 2019. Results Report. Professionality Index Measurement, State Civil Apparatus, 2018. Jakarta.

Table 3.12 provides more detail on the variation in professionalism among national-level organizations. The highest-scoring ministries are the Ministry of Social Affairs, the Coordinating Ministry of Maritime Affairs, and the Coordinating Ministry of Human Development and Culture. The lowest-performing are the Ministry of Law and Human Rights (with very low reporting), Ministry of Environment and Forests, and the Ministry of Youth and Sports.

Table 3.12: Performance of Civil Servants in National Departments, 2018

Agency	Percentage of Respondents (%)	Average Qualification	Average Competence	Average Performance	Discipline	IP	Category
Ministry of State Secretariat	80.60	13.00	36.00	25.00	5.00	79.00	Moderate
Cabinet Secretariat	1.68	15.00	28.00	25.00	5.00	73.00	Moderate
Ministry of National Development Planning/Bappenas	0.50	16.00	26.00	22.00	5.00	69.00	Low
Coordinating Ministry for Maritime Affairs and Investment	40.80	18.00	34.00	25.00	5.00	82.00	High
Ministry of Transportation	27.45	10.00	21.00	26.00	5.00	62.00	Low
Marine and Fisheries Ministry	73.61	13.00	20.00	25.00	5.00	63.00	Low
Ministry of Energy and Mineral Resources	38.94	13.00	20.00	24.00	5.00	62.00	Low
Ministry of Tourism	30.78	14.00	17.00	25.00	5.00	61.00	Low
Coordinating Ministry for Political, Legal and Security	1.89	16.00	25.00	22.00	5.00	68.00	Low
Ministry of Internal Affairs	100.00	15.00	20.00	24.00	5.00	64.00	Low
Ministry of Foreign Affairs	96.01	16.00	20.00	25.00	5.00	66.00	Low
Ministry of Defense	4.21	10.00	25.00	22.00	5.00	62.00	Low
Ministry of Law and Human Rights	1.36	11.00	12.00	24.00	5.00	52.00	Very low
Ministry of Communication and Informatics	14.41	14.00	21.00	21.00	5.00	61.00	Low
Ministry of Administrative Reform and Bureaucratic Reform	1.02	16.00	30.00	28.00	5.00	79.00	Moderate
Coordinating Ministry for Economic Affairs	0.86	16.00	26.00	22.00	5.00	69.00	Low
Ministry of Finance	98.03	16.00	31.00	26.00	5.00	78.00	Moderate
Ministry of State-Owned Enterprises	11.30	15.00	31.00	27.00	5.00	78.00	Moderate
Ministry of Cooperatives and Small and Medium Enterprises	0.40	15.00	18.00	25.00	5.00	63.00	Lowß
Ministry of Industry	94.63	14.00	20.00	23.00	5.00	62.00	Low
Ministry of Trade	90.43	15.00	19.00	25.00	5.00	64.00	Low

Continued next page

Table 3.12 continued

Ministry of Agriculture	0.95	13.00	26.00	22.00	5.00	66.00	Low
Ministry of Labor	91.21	14.00	29.00	22.00	5.00	70.00	Low
Minister for Public Works and Human Settlements	55.03	12.00	19.00	25.00	5.00	61.00	Low
Ministry of Environment and Forests	98.08	11.00	15.00	25.00	5.00	56.00	Very low
Ministry of Agricultural and Spatial Planning / National Land Agency	7.22	12.00	20.00	25.00	5.00	62.00	Low
Coordinating Ministry of Human Development and Culture	0.92	15.00	40.00	25.00	5.00	85.00	High
Ministry of Religion	24.20	14.00	21.00	23.00	5.00	63.00	Low
Ministry of Health	0.11	15.00	18.00	24.00	5.00	62.00	Low
Ministry of Social Affairs	0.39	17.00	36.00	25.00	5.00	83.00	High
Ministry of Women's Empowerment and Child Protection	0.38	15.00	20.00	25.00	5.00	65.00	Low
Ministry of Culture, Primary and Secondary Education	99.18	13.00	20.00	25.00	5.00	63.00	Low
Ministry of Research Technology and Higher Education	58.18	17.00	15.00	25.00	5.00	62.00	Low
Ministry of Youth and Sports	60.87	13.00	14.00	24.00	5.00	56.00	Very low
Ministry of Rural, Rural Development and Transmigration	0.06	15.00	20.00	25.00	5.00	65.00	Low

IP = Indeks Profesional/Professionalism Index.
Source: Author based on BKN. 2019. Results Report. Professionality Index Measurement, State Civil Apparatus, 2018. Jakarta.

The low response rate during the collection of input data for the Professionalism Index reveals an ongoing challenge for Indonesia's human resources management in the public sector: while administrative data that are useful for human resources management are being collected, such efforts, at times, lack standardization, comprehensiveness, and subsequent analysis to aid managerial decision-making.

A recent report by the OECD and ADB (2019) reviewed a series of public sector capacities and practices, including public sector data availability and accessibility. While Indonesia compares favorably on these dimensions with other Southeast Asian countries and even with the OECD average, it lags behind East Asian nations like Japan and the Republic of Korea (Figure 3.7), and it does not regularly collect, aggregate, or standardize key employee performance data at the central government level (Figure 3.8). While some ministries utilize staff surveys to collect actionable data for human resources planning, the Indonesian government has no centralized system in place to deploy comprehensive civil servant surveys across the breadth of the civil service (OECD and ADB 2019).

Capacity and Skills | 25

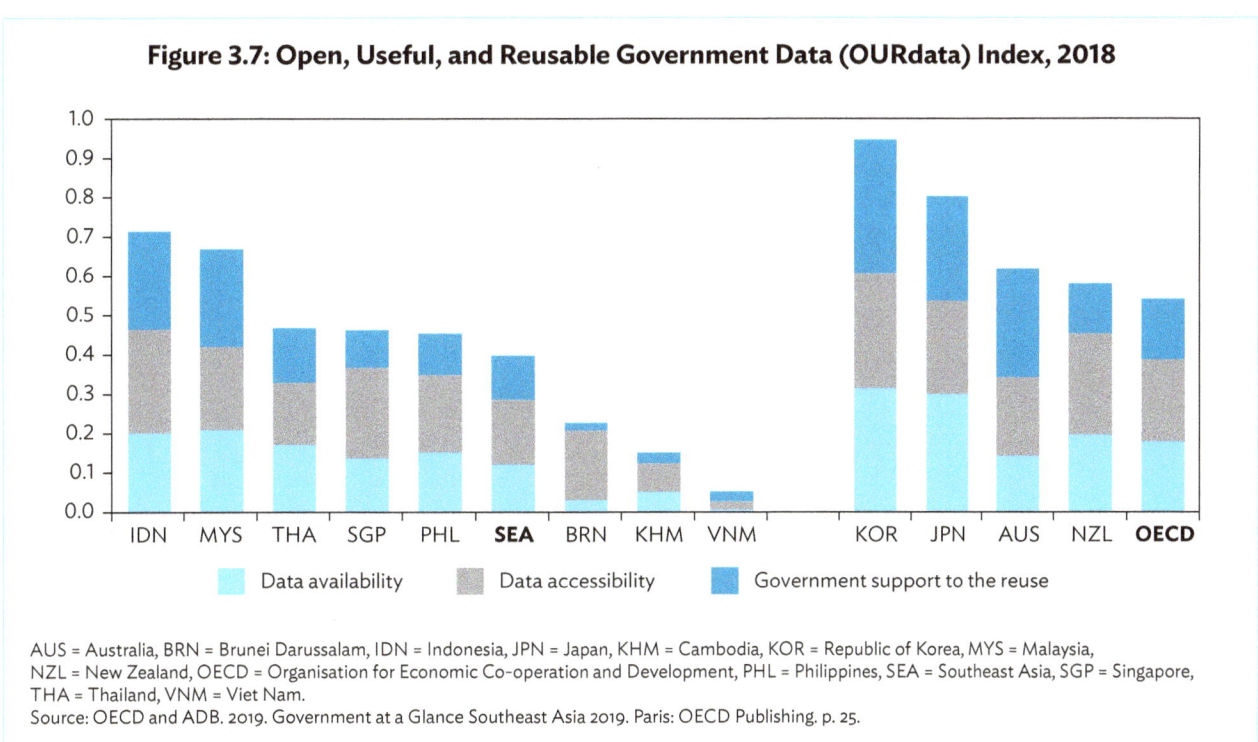

Figure 3.7: Open, Useful, and Reusable Government Data (OURdata) Index, 2018

AUS = Australia, BRN = Brunei Darussalam, IDN = Indonesia, JPN = Japan, KHM = Cambodia, KOR = Republic of Korea, MYS = Malaysia, NZL = New Zealand, OECD = Organisation for Economic Co-operation and Development, PHL = Philippines, SEA = Southeast Asia, SGP = Singapore, THA = Thailand, VNM = Viet Nam.
Source: OECD and ADB. 2019. Government at a Glance Southeast Asia 2019. Paris: OECD Publishing. p. 25.

Figure 3.8: Collection and Aggregation of Employee Performance Data, 2018

	Collected/aggregated centrally and updated regularly	Collected and held at Ministry level, standardised	Collected by ministries/ agencies, not standardised
Brunei Darussalam	●	○	○
Cambodia	○	○	●
Indonesia	○	○	●
Lao PDR	○	○	●
Malaysia	●	○	○
Philippines	●	○	○
Singapore	○	●	○
Thailand	○	●	○
Viet Nam	●	○	○
SEA Total	4	2	3
Australia	○	○	●
Republic of Korea	○	○	●
Japan	○	●	○
New Zealand	○	○	●
OECD Total	12	4	14

● Yes   ○ No

Lao PDR = Lao People's Democratic Republic, OECD = Organisation for Economic Co-operation and Development, SEA = Southeast Asia.
Source: OECD and ADB. 2019. Government at a Glance Southeast Asia 2019. Paris: OECD Publishing. p. 79.

Academic research literature has also attempted to generate more comprehensive aggregate metrics for civil service effectiveness that are a function of competence and skill in the civil service. For example, the International Civil Service Effectiveness Index (InCiSE) (2019) is an effort to provide a comprehensive assessment of civil service effectiveness based on 12 input indicators that aim to measure capabilities, crisis and risk management, digital services, fiscal and financial management, human resources management, inclusiveness, integrity, openness, policy making, procurement, regulation, and tax administration.[6] Currently, Indonesia has not been assessed as part of the InCiSE Index. Efforts to provide data for Indonesia along the 12 dimensions of the InCiSE Index would be worthwhile and help to assess the overall state of Indonesia's civil service.

Other common indices of government effectiveness typically rely on expert surveys and aggregate data. Table 3.13 provides an overview of Indonesia's position within the Association of Southeast Asian Nations (ASEAN) on the World Bank's Ease of Doing Business Ranking (2019), Transparency International's Corruption Perception Index (2018), and the World Bank's Government Effectiveness Index (2017). Overall, Indonesia displays middling performance across these three indicators relative to other ASEAN members. Indonesia is outperformed by Singapore, Malaysia, Thailand, Brunei Darussalam, and Viet Nam in the Ease of Doing Business Ranking; by Brunei Darussalam, Malaysia, and Singapore in corruption perceptions; and by Brunei Darussalam, Malaysia, Singapore, and Thailand in government effectiveness.

Table 3.13: Government Performance Indices

Country	Ease of Doing Business 2019	Corruption Perception Index 2018	Government Effectiveness 2017
Brunei Darussalam	66 out of 190	31 out of 180	1.14
Cambodia	144 out of 190	161 out of 180	-0.66
Indonesia	**73 out of 190**	**89 out of 180**	**0.04**
Lao PDR	154 out of 190	132 out of 180	-0.36
Malaysia	12 out of 190	61 out of 180	0.84
Myanmar	165 out of 190	132 out of 180	-1.05
Philippines	95 out of 190	99 out of 180	-0.06
Singapore	2 out of 190	3 out of 180	2.21
Thailand	21 out of 190	99 out of 180	0.38
Viet Nam	70 out of 190	117 out of 180	0.00

Lao PDR = Lao People's Democratic Republic.
Source: Author.

In total, using educational attainment and BKN's Professionalism Index to assess the competence and skill of Indonesia's civil service reveals room for improvement. Indonesia's civil service as a whole does not have the desired level of competence across all government units. There are especially stark differences across central versus regional government units and across the geography of Indonesia's provincial and district governments. Moreover, it remains unclear if existing recruitment practices and on-the-job training programs are adequately structured to deliver the required skills for the future needs of Indonesia's civil service.

---

[6] Data sources for these dimensions are public opinion surveys, enterprise surveys, social surveys, government administrative data, and OECD surveys. Note that this type of approach does not utilize individual-level civil servant data.

A Deeper Look at the Education Sector

Given the importance of skills acquisition for the Indonesian civil service and the workforce writ large, it is particularly important to consider the quality of service delivery and the challenges presented by the education sector.

Over the last 20 years, Indonesia's education system has changed substantially. In the past, the central government bore direct responsibility for Indonesian schools and teachers. Teaching as a profession lacked systematic and clear standards, offered fairly low salaries, and hiring was often driven by personal relationships (Kristiansen and Ramli 2006). This status quo was upended by decentralization reforms in 2001 and the 2005 Teacher Law. The decentralization reforms transferred authority over schools and teachers to the district level, making local governments responsible for the provision of primary and secondary education. The Teacher Law introduced several elements of professionalization, including minimum educational entry standards for teachers, additional professionalization requirements, and better salaries. The reforms also included a constitutional amendment that requires the government to spend at least 20% of its fiscal resources in the education sector. This surge in fiscal resources led to a substantial increase in the number of teachers, creating one of the lowest student–teacher ratios in the developing world (Cerdan-Infantes et al. 2013).

Despite the dramatic increase in fiscal, bureaucratic, and personnel inputs to the education system, the quality of the educational outputs improved only slightly. Based on the 2012 Programme for International Student Assessment's internationally standardized tests of math, science, and reading skills among 15-year-old students in 65 participating countries, Indonesia ranked 60th in reading skills and 64th in math and science (Chang et al. 2013).

An important feature of Indonesia's public education system is the formal authority district governments have over the provision of primary and secondary education. While the Ministry of Education and the Ministry of Religious Affairs have some oversight role over public and religious schools, respectively, district governments enjoy considerable latitude in the hiring, placement, and management of over 3 million teachers across 330,000 schools, affecting the educational outcome of 59 million students (Cerdan-Infantes et al. 2013).

This generates a number of new challenges, ranging from the varying capacity of district governments to effectively provide educational services, to the difficulty of central government institutions in exerting effective top-down control and oversight. For example, the issue of teacher hiring starkly illustrates the challenges of civil service management when authority structures are decentralized.

Districts can hire teachers as permanent civil servants (PNS), but teachers must fulfill certain minimum standards, pass a civil service exam, and comply with the standards set by civil service rules and regulations. In addition to the stringent entry requirements, the central government also set strict hiring quotas on the total number of new civil service teaching jobs. While the central government can set standards and enforce hiring quotas, district governments have actual authority over hiring and can choose to hire teachers on a short-term basis under the category of contract teachers (non-PNS). Contract teachers are hired directly at the district- or school-level and are paid 10%–50% of the typical civil service salary, without permanent contracts. From 2006 to 2010, 377,000 new teachers were hired, 60% of them as contract teachers (Cerdan-Infantes et al. 2013). As a result of the substantial increase in the number of teachers, Indonesia is one of the countries with the lowest student–teacher ratios, very likely representing an inefficient overinvestment into the teaching force. The influx of teaching personnel is also distributed unevenly across Indonesian districts, exacerbating geographic inequities across the country (Chang et al. 2013).

Several factors can explain the massive wave of teacher hiring. For example, fiscal incentives inherent to the intergovernmental transfer system reward district governments with higher allocations for a greater number of civil servants. Similarly, the central government's Operational School Assistance Program (BOS) subsidizes the school-level hiring of contract teachers. This means that principals, typically under the direction of a district head, can use fiscal resources to hire contract teachers without affecting the district budget. School-level hiring is also exempted from a number of regulations, making the process particularly susceptible to political patronage.

Research suggests that the increase in contract teacher hiring is also partially driven by local political considerations. Pierskalla and Sacks (2019) find that contract teacher hiring increased following the introduction of direct elections, with spikes during election years. Handing out teaching jobs as a political reward has become more common now that district heads are elected directly, since they have control over the local education department (Chang et al. 2013, p. 173).

In addition to central–local conflict over hiring priorities, the central government is facing some challenges in its attempt to increase skills acquisition and professionalize the teaching force. Most importantly, the 2005 Teacher Law created a high-powered certification program for civil service teachers. The certification scheme offers teachers the opportunity to be officially certified if they can present a document showing that they hold a 4-year degree and submit a teaching portfolio (or alternatively, completion of a special training workshop). Upon certification, teachers are given a special allowance, nearly doubling their effective salary. The program was implemented in phases from 2006 to 2015 and resulted in a large number of teachers certified, creating a substantial financial burden on the government. The program is a unique intervention to professionalize Indonesia's civil service by linking high-powered financial incentives with concrete civil servant behaviors. Despite the program's well-intentioned objective, however, early evidence of the scheme's outcome has been disappointing. A high-quality randomized-controlled trial evaluation of the program revealed increased job satisfaction for teachers but no measurable gain in student learning (de Ree et al. 2018).

In summary, Indonesia's public education sector has gone through numerous changes since democratization in 1999. On the one hand, decentralization, national-level regulatory changes, and a large influx of fiscal resources have modernized Indonesia's teaching profession. On the other hand, substantial governance challenges remain, with little evidence that reforms have improved the actual quality of educational services. Moreover, politicization of the civil service has exacerbated the deleterious influences of clientelism, patronage, and corruption.

The Role of Gender and Diversity

Civil service organizations are not often descriptively representative (in terms of gender, class, ethnicity, caste, or religion) of the populations they serve (Rogger 2017; UN Women 2015). This is particularly true for civil service leadership positions in Indonesia and Southeast Asia in general (OECD and ADB 2019, p. 9). A growing body of research indicates that this may have detrimental consequences for the performance of the state. A larger share of women and minorities in public office (elected or appointed) have been found to have an effect on the quality of public goods provision; the types of public goods provided, including goods and services that meet the needs of the most vulnerable populations; the bureaucracy's ability to understand the needs of their clients; the quality of political leaders; and the degree of corruption in the bureaucracy (Bhavnani and Lee 2019, Bradbury and Kellough 2011; Rasul and Rogger 2015; Herring 2009; Krislov 2012; Pepinsky et al. 2017; Duflo 2012; Vernby 2013; Besley et al. 2017; Brollo and Troiano 2016; Gulzar, Haas, and Pasquale 2018; Chin and Prakash 2011; Clayton and Zetterberg 2018; Pande 2003; Park 2013).

Better representation of women and other underrepresented groups also shapes the people's perceptions of the state, especially with regard to the trustworthiness of civil servants. A civil service whose employees share ascriptive characteristics such as ethnicity, gender, language, or culture with citizens can dramatically improve the citizens' evaluations of interactions with the state (Krislov 2012; Theobald and Haider-Markel 2009; Riccucci et al. 2014; Mettler 1998; Barnes et al. 2018).

Stronger descriptive representation also amplifies the depth of embeddedness of civil servants in their local communities, allowing those in the frontline to frame their messages and perform their tasks in culturally appropriate ways, and thus raising their effectiveness. This also increases the probability that clients will adopt their providers' recommendations (such as in the health care sector) or result in citizens' greater understanding of eligibility requirements (Tendler and Freedheim 1994). Citizens who perceive their civil servants to be trustworthy are also more likely to view the government more generally as legitimate and in turn more likely to quasi-voluntarily comply with government rules and regulations like paying taxes, which enhances the state's capacity in the long run (Levi and Sacks 2009).

Traditionally, Indonesia's civil service has been dominated by men and Muslim civil servants from Java, especially among echelon-level employees. The majority of women in civil service are employed as teachers and health care workers. While overall female representation in the civil service has improved since the 1970s, a pattern of male dominance has a long tradition and reflects societal norms and biases (Azmi et al. 2012). Indonesia's labor market as a whole is biased against women (Wright and Crocket Tellei 1993).[7]

Recent surveys of women in the civil service indicate that they are often overlooked for promotions or decide to reject offers for promotion because they are required to relocate to remote provinces (Azmi et al. 2012). Also, while women can request to be reassigned to follow their husbands, this often requires a demotion in job responsibilities. Men on the other hand cannot request to relocate with their wives, which often gives rise to inequities in who gets promoted to a higher-level position via rotation to peripheral areas (Azmi et al. 2012). Women civil servants are also rarely perceived to be the main breadwinners for their households; but they are often expected to put their family over career aspirations. These cultural factors have inhibited their career advancement.

Table 3.14 shows the breakdown by gender across the echelon hierarchy of Indonesia's civil service. At the level of functional employees, Indonesia's civil service is balanced, which is not surprising, since women have good representation among teachers and health care workers. Across all echelon levels though, women are underrepresented, their share ranging from only 16%–35%. Women are particularly underrepresented at echelon level 2, with only 16% of employees—a troubling thought especially because this is the pool of Indonesia's future top-level civil servants.

Table 3.14: Share of Female Civil Servants by Echelon, 2015

Echelon Level	Share of Female Civil Servants
Echelon 1	0.28
Echelon 2	0.16
Echelon 3	0.21
Echelon 4	0.35
Echelon 5	0.31
Functional	0.52

Source: Author.

---

[7] While political reforms introduced gender quotas for female candidates in legislative elections (Shair-Rosenfield 2012), quotas have not been introduced in the civil service.

Non-Muslim representation in the civil service is higher than the overall population share (87.8% of the general population identifies as Muslim). Table 3.15 reports the share of non-Muslim civil servants in the functional and echelon levels. The share of non-Muslim civil servants is lowest among echelon 1 employees at 11%.

Table 3.15: Share of Religious Minority Civil Servants by Echelon, 2015

Echelon Level	Share Minority Civil Servants
Echelon 1	0.11
Echelon 2	0.21
Echelon 3	0.21
Echelon 4	0.19
Echelon 5	0.14
Functional	0.18

Source: Author.

The share of female civil servants not only varies along the echelon hierarchy but even more so across national ministries and district governments. Tables 3.16 and 3.17 present the share of female civil servants for the top-10 and bottom-10 national departments. Organizations like the Ministry of Health and the Ministry of Women Empowerment and Child Protection have more than 60% female employees. In contrast, the Ministry of Finance and the Ministry of Law and Human Rights have only about 26% female employees. This indicates substantial variation in work environments for female civil servants.

Table 3.16: Top-10 National Departments by Share of Female Civil Servants, 2015

Department	Share of Female Civil Servants
National Agency of Drug and Food Control	0.72
Indonesian National Military Headquarters	0.62
Ministry of Health	0.61
Ministry of Women Empowerment and Child Protection	0.60
Indonesian National Police	0.54
National Anti-Narcotics Agency	0.53
Indonesian Financial Transaction Report and Analysis Center	0.53
National Library of the Republic of Indonesia	0.52
Ministry of Religious Affairs	0.50
Ministry of Defense	0.49

Source: Author.

Table 3.17: Bottom-10 National Departments by Share of Female Civil Servants, 2015

Department	Share of Female Civil Servants
Agency for the Assessment and Application of Technology	0.26
Ministry of Law and Human Rights	0.26
Ministry of Finance	0.26
Coordinating Ministry of Maritime Affairs	0.25
Ministry of Transportation	0.21
Batam Indonesia Free Zone Authority	0.20
Secretariat General of Corruption Eradication Commission	0.16
National Search and Rescue Agency	0.16
State Civil Apparatus Commission	0.13
Secretariat General of Commission for the Supervision of Business Competition	0.00

Source: Author.

The variation is even more extreme across district governments. Tables 3.18 and 3.19 depict the share of female civil servants in the top-10 and bottom-10 district governments. Ambon, Pekanbaru, Palembang, and Padang are among the districts with the highest share of female civil servants, comprising about 70% of the civil service workforce (and partially reflecting distinct local gender attitudes). In the bottom-10 districts in Papua, such as Puncak, Yahukimo, and Tolikara, women make up only about 25% of the civil service workforce.

Table 3.18: Top-10 Districts by Share of Female Civil Servants, 2015

District Government	Share of Female Civil Servants
Government of Ambon City	0.71
Government of Pekanbaru City	0.70
Government of Palembang City	0.70
Government of Padang City	0.69
Government of Minahasa	0.69
Government of Padang Pariaman District	0.69
Government of Deli Serdang District	0.68
Government of Agam District	0.68
Government of Tanah Datar District	0.67
Government of North Minahasa District	0.67

Source: Author.

Table 3.19: Bottom-10 Districts by Share of Female Civil Servants, 2015

District Government	Share of Female Civil Servants
Government of Paniai District	0.29
Government of South Manokwari District	0.28
Government of Intan Jaya District	0.28
Government of Pegunungan Bintang District	0.28
Government of Lanny Jaya District	0.26
Government of Puncak Jaya District	0.26
Government of Puncak District	0.25
Government of Tolikara District	0.23
Government of Yahukimo District	0.23
Government of Pegunungan Arfak District	0.09

Source: Author.

An analysis of promotion patterns in Indonesia's civil service reveals that female civil servants are promoted at a lower rate than male civil servants (Pierskalla et al. 2019). This disadvantage for female civil servants holds, even when controlling for educational attainment and other characteristics (Pierskalla et al. 2019). Moreover, the gender limitation has worsened over the last 20 years, suggesting the emergence of additional challenges for female civil servants (Pierskalla et al. 2019). Qualitative research on the chances of promotion for female civil servants in Bali further substantiates the constraints on their career advancement (Krissetyanti, Prasojo, and Kasim 2017).

To reap the potential benefits of a diverse civil service and in effect raise its descriptive representation, the Indonesian government could more seriously engage with female and minority civil servants.

4. GOVERNANCE AND INSTITUTIONAL CONTEXT

The civil service as a whole operates under the supervision and guidance of three national departments and agencies: the state Ministry for Administrative and Bureaucratic Reform (MenPAN), the National Institute of Public Administration (LAN), and the National Civil Service Agency (BKN). As a result of the Civil Service Reform Law (Law No. 5/2014), the Civil Service Commission of Indonesia was created, consisting of seven members from government, academia, and civil society, with oversight authority over the implementation of the ethics code.

These national-level institutions have some control over essential human resources and management functions but share responsibilities with line ministries and regional government bodies. In the areas of the general management of pay systems, flexibility of working conditions, allocation of budgetary resources between payroll and other expenses, performance appraisal, performance pay, control over the number of positions, and recruitment into the civil service, line ministries share authority with MenPAN, BKN, and LAN (OECD and ADB 2019, p. 77). Especially in the area of recruitment, local and regional government units exercise substantial latitude with limited control mechanisms for central government actors (see more on decentralization in the next section).

Recruitment Process for Civil Service Applicants

Civil service is a highly sought-after career path in Indonesia, and many applications are received for each available position. To be selected, civil servant applicants have to pass an entrance exam, which in the past has been administered in paper form and as a consequence plagued by corrupt practices, including scams for preparatory courses, leveraging of familial connections, cheating, and the outright purchase of civil service positions (Kristiansen and Ramli 2006; Tidey 2012; World Bank 2018a; Blunt, Turner, and Lindroth 2012a, 2012b).

There are several stages in the recruitment process. First, applicants are screened for meeting the initial requirements of educational attainment and work experience. Then, applicants sit for a written entrance exam, comprising a general intelligence test, a personality test, and questions covering national loyalty. Finally, candidates have to pass additional subject-specific entry exams for specific ministries. In 2013, BKN introduced the use of a new computer-assisted entrance exam for civil servants. Initially, this change was not adopted uniformly across all levels of government, but early impressions were positive, suggesting increased transparency and credibility of the process (World Bank 2018a). Subsequently, the government opted for uniform use of the new entrance exam in 2014 but actual use has been lagging, partially because of the moratorium on hiring. Despite the widespread concern about non-meritocratic recruitment, Pierskalla et al. (2019) provide descriptive evidence that the profiles, in terms of gender or educational attainment of incoming civil servant cohorts, have not changed substantially over the last decade, which which is likely explained by the high ratio of applications to open positions. A high degree of consistency in basic demographic characteristics of incoming cohorts does not indicate the existence or absence of corruption in the recruitment process, given the large number of applicants and that the ability to engage in corruption may be positively correlated with skill, ability, or educational attainment (Weaver 2020). While the new computer-assisted entrance exam seems like a step in the right direction, it remains unclear whether recruitment practices in general truly serve the current and future needs of the Indonesian civil service. Structuring the selection into public service has important consequences for the type of individuals that attempt to become civil servants, their underlying competency, public sector motivation, and susceptibility for corruption (for an overview of related literature, see Hasnain, Manning, and Pierskalla 2014).

The hierarchy of the civil service is structured along two separate dimensions: echelon level and *golongan* (rank). A civil servant attains the echelon level as a result of merit-based promotions, signifying advancement in managerial responsibility. Table 4.1 lists existing echelon ranks, ranging from level 4 to the top levels of 1a and 1b.[8] At the district level, a typical echelon 4 civil servant would be the *kecamatan* (head of a sub-division) or the head of a technical implementation unit. The national-level echelon 4 would be composed of section heads. At the top of the hierarchy, levels 1a and 1b include director generals, heads of agencies, and the primary auditor or regional secretaries.

All civil servants begin their career as nonstructural employees. They advance through the echelon hierarchy based on minimum requirements, work experience and *golongan* (rank), past job performance as captured by annual performance reviews, and the successful recommendation of a promotion panel. As of now, there is no mid-career entry on the echelon scale, i.e., civil servants have to advance internally along the hierarchy and outsiders from the private sector cannot enter directly and assume a high-level echelon position. Recently, some have suggested the use of contract employees from the private sector to fill certain positions on the echelon hierarchy (Jakarta Post 2018). President Widodo also recently introduced a plan for the reform of the echelon hierarchy, collapsing it into two ranks only (Reformasi Weekly 2019). This focus on career progression from within the ranks of civil servants and the lack of lateral entry by professionals from outside the public sector is typical for governments in Southeast Asia as a whole (OECD and ADB 2019, p. 81).

For internal career advancement, performance reviews play an important procedural role. In the past, performance reviews used vague and subjective criteria (Nuswantoro 2017). Changes to regulations in 2011 introduced new individual performance reviews that were meant to more clearly align civil servant performance with the organization's goals (Nuswantoro 2017). A recent study of the new performance review system identifies three persistent issues: (i) individual civil servant feedback remains vague and, at times, expresses bias by superiors; (ii) the performance review is not effectively linked to meaningful rewards or sanctions; and (iii) the new performance review has increased administrative burdens (Nuswantoro 2017).

A promotion panel consisting of superior officers is required to evaluate candidates for higher-level positions based on meritocratic principles. At the district-level, elected district heads play a powerful role in promotion decisions, potentially creating an opening for the politicization of bureaucratic procedures (Berenschot 2018). A recent World Bank report, analyzing past promotion decisions, found that educational attainment is predictive of advancement on the echelon scale (Sacks and Pierskalla 2018). The premium attached to educational attainment has also substantially increased since democratization in 1999 (Pierskalla 2019). At the same time, there is evidence of sustained discrimination against women and religious minorities (Pierskalla et al.

---

[8] Echelon level 5 is deprecated since Indonesia's Law No. 5 in 2014 on Civil Service Apparatus. Nonetheless, there are still actively employed civil servants in that echelon level.

Table 4.1: Echelon Levels in Indonesia's Civil Service

Echelon	Department of Central Agencies/National Level	Province Level	District Level
1a	Secretary general, director general, secretary, principal secretary, head of agency, inspector general, superintendent, president director, primary auditor, deputy general prosecutor, solicitor general, deputy, deputy secretary of the Cabinet		
1b	Staff member	Regional secretary	
2a	Head of bureau, head of center, deputy assistant	Assistant, expert staff of governor, secretary of Parliament (DPRD), head of service, head of agency, inspector, director of Regional General Hospital Class A	Regional secretary
2b		Head of bureau, director of Regional Public Hospital Class B, deputy director of Class A General Hospital, director of Special Class A Hospital	Assistant, expert staff of regent/mayor, secretary of Parliament (DPRD), head of service, head of agency, director of Regional General Hospital Class A and B
3a	Head of division, head of sector, head of sub-directorate	Head of office, head of section, secretary of office/agency/inspectorate, chief of field, assistant inspector, director of Public Hospital Class C, director of Special Hospital Class B, deputy director of Class B Public Hospital, vice director of Special Class A Hospital, head of Technical Implementation Unit Service	Head of office, subdistrict head, head of section, secretary of office/agency/inspectorate, assistant inspector, director of Public Hospital Class C, director of Special Hospital Class B, deputy director of Class A and B Public Hospital, deputy director of Class A Special Hospital
3b		Head of division at Regional Hospital, head of sector at Regional Hospital	Head of division at the office and agency, head of division and head of sector at the Regional General Hospital, director of D Class Regional Hospital, secretary of sub-district
4a	Head of subdivision, head of subsector, head of section	Head of subdivision, head of subsector, head of section	Urban village head, head of subdivision, head of subsector, head of section, head of Technical Implementation Unit Service and Agency
4b			Secretary of urban village, section head of sub-district, head of the subdivision unit, head of subdivision at the district secretary, head of administration of Vocational Secondary School
5a	Head of affairs		Head of administration of First Level Continuation, head of administration of Senior High School

Source: Author.

2019). Pierskalla (2019) also provides evidence that since 1999 promotions have started to cluster during election years, suggesting an increased politicization of the promotion process. Qualitative field research by Berenschot (2018) also suggests that local district heads leverage their control over the civil service to build a loyal political machine among civil servants to advance their electoral goals.

Table 4.2 depicts the distribution of civil servants across echelon levels, disaggregated by gender. The vast majority (73.07%) of echelon-level civil servants are employed at level 4. Only about 5% of echelon-level civil servants attain the rank of echelon 1 or 2. Across echelon ranks, there exists an obvious gender disparity. Women make up only 32.91% of all echelon-level employees—at the top echelon 1 level, there are more than three times women as many men. At echelon 2, there are nearly six times as many men as women.

Table 4.2: Civil Servants by Echelon Level, 2018

Echelon Level	Men	%	Women	%	Total	%
Echelon 1	735	0.16	233	0.05	968	0.21
Echelon 2	19,167	4.15	3,358	0.73	22,525	4.88
Echelon 3	77,427	16.78	23,349	5.06	100,776	21.84
Echelon 4	212,295	46.00	124,922	27.07	337,217	73.07
Total	**309,624**	**67.09**	**151,862**	**32.91**	**461,486**	**100**

Source: Author based on BKN. 2018. Civil Servant Statistics Book December 2018. Jakarta. p. 33.

Civil servants are also classified by *golongan* (rank). Rank is another dimension of hierarchical advancement for civil servants (with implications for salary levels). Advancement in rank is determined by educational attainment and work experience. There are four broad ranks: 1, 2, 3, and 4. Table 4.3 provides information on the distribution of civil servants across ranks, by gender. Only 1.14% of civil servants attain rank 1 (1.02% men, 0.12% women), 18.98% for rank 2 (11.52% men, 7.46% women), 54.3% for rank 3 (24.75% men, 29.54% women), and 25.59% for rank 4 (12.2% men, 13.39% women).

Table 4.3: Civil Servants by Golongan (Rank), 2018

Golongan	Men	%	Women	%	Total	%
Golongan 1	42,516	1.02	5,054	0.12	47,570	1.14
Golongan 2	482,062	11.52	312,224	7.46	794,286	18.98
Golongan 3	1,036,105	24.75	1,236,480	29.54	2,272,585	54.30
Golongan 4	510,627	12.20	560,435	13.39	1,071,062	25.59
Total	**2,071,310**	**49.49**	**2,114,193**	**50.51**	**4,185,503**	**100**

Source: Author based on BKN. 2018. Civil Servant Statistics Book December 2018. Jakarta. p. 35.

Figure 4.1 shows the distribution of ranks for central and regional civil servants, while Table 4.4 disaggregates the distribution of ranks across age brackets in the civil service.

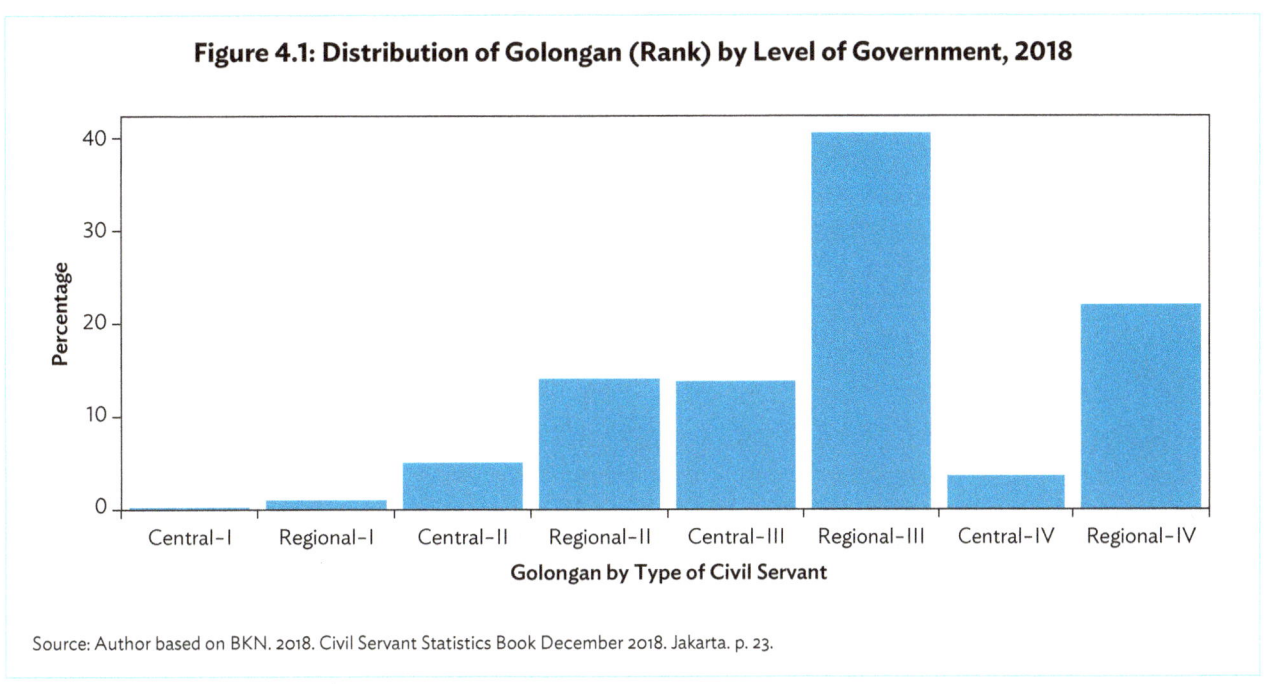

Figure 4.1: Distribution of Golongan (Rank) by Level of Government, 2018

Source: Author based on BKN. 2018. Civil Servant Statistics Book December 2018. Jakarta. p. 23.

Table 4.4: Golongan (Rank) by Age Bracket, 2018

Age Bracket	Golongan 1	Golongan 2	Golongan 3	Golongan 4	Total
18–20	0	8,910	5	0	8,915
21–25	0	30,120	14,845	0	44,965
26–30	0	61,837	86,398	7	148,242
31–35	4,700	137,816	358,401	1,277	502,194
36–40	6,611	160,690	475,446	18,294	661,041
41–45	9,189	128,801	403,409	58,665	600,064
46–50	11,525	128,394	426,336	194,225	760,480
51–55	10,975	106,534	375,539	409,930	902,978
56–60	4,570	31,184	129,889	377,971	543,614
> 60	0	0	2,317	10,693	13,010
Total	**47,570**	**794,286**	**2,272,585**	**1,071,062**	**4,185,503**

Source: Author based on BKN. 2018. Civil Servant Statistics Book December 2018. Jakarta. p. 34.

Both echelon level and rank are important inputs for civil servant salaries. Overall, salaries are determined by strict schedules that account for the level of responsibility, local cost of living, and job type. Despite the popularity of civil service jobs, the overall monetary compensation is comparatively low for higher-level jobs in the bureaucracy (Tjiptoherijanto 2014). A number of official and unofficial allowances and nonpecuniary benefits supplement their basic salary (e.g., special allotments of rice, holiday bonuses, access to insurance benefits and retirement plans). A recent comparative study of public sector employment, drawing on representative labor market surveys across several countries, reveals that Indonesian civil servants as a whole enjoy a substantial wage premium over the private sector (Finan, Olken, and Pande 2015). Notably, high pecuniary incentives in civil service recruitment may crowd out job applications by individuals with high public sector motivation (for a review of the literature, see Hasnain, Manning, and Pierskalla 2014). A study of Indonesian subjects from the public and private sector finds that pro-socially motivated individuals exert more effort in pro-social tasks, but higher salaries attract individuals with low social motivation (Banuri and Keefer 2016). While recent regulatory changes have increased the flexibility to experiment with performance pay elements, Indonesia as a whole is below the OECD and Southeast Asian average in terms of its utilization of performance pay elements in the civil service (see OECD and ADB 2019, p. 32).

Official civil service reforms after democratization have only slowly impacted the actual operation of Indonesia's bureaucracy. Reform Law No. 43/1999 allowed for increased flexibility to supplement civil servant salaries, depending on the local cost of living, and codified a merit-based personnel management approach. Presidential Regulation No. 81 of 2010 outlined in more detail a "Grand Design," covering eight areas of bureaucratic reform: organization, business processes, human resources management, supervision, accountability, public service delivery, and culture. Subsequently, several well-known civil service experts and reformers have been appointed to high-level positions at the National Institute of Public Administration (LAN) and the Ministry for Administrative and Bureaucratic Reform (MenPAN).

The more ambitious Law No. 5/2014 laid the regulatory groundwork for the modernization of the civil service, in particular by codifying the assessment of job performance and merit principles, but substantive change has nonetheless been slow. Under the 2014 law, promotions to high-level structural positions are meant to occur within an open and competitive process that rewards competence, education, training, work experience, and integrity, and are not supposed to be based on age, gender, religion, origin, marital status, disabilities, or political affiliation. Several bottlenecks have slowed the adoption of merit practices in the promotion practices for higher-level positions, such as the lack of certified assessment centers and assessors for competency testing or continuing political interventions in the promotion process (Dwiputrianti 2018). Despite the mandate of Law No. 5/2014 recruitment across central and regional government units to higher-level positions often violates the principles of open recruitment, awarding positions without truly competitive selection procedures and even the outright buying of positions (Suwitri et al. 2019; Kristiansen and Ramli 2006). The newly created Civil Service Commission has issued warnings about these violations but has no formal authority over provincial- and district-level selection procedures (Suwitri et al. 2019). One member of the Civil Service Commission estimates that 90% of civil service organizations are involved in the practice of buying and selling of positions and specifically identified the Ministries of Education, Health, and Religion as particularly affected (Suwitri et al. 2019).

Even so, specific progress has been made in some ministries. The reform effort by Sri Mulyani Indrawati during her first stint as Minister of Finance from 2005 to 2010 resulted in considerable improvement in the internal operations of the ministry. The Ministry of Finance had been struggling with recruited skilled individuals as a consequence of low pay at higher echelon positions, overlapping responsibilities of internal units, unclear task assignments, and high degrees of corruption in, for example customs and excise administration (LaForge 2016). With sufficient political backing and available fiscal resources for reform, Sri Mulyani made several sweeping changes in the ministry. She created new, high-level units to assist her reform efforts and clarified the portfolios and responsibilities of high-echelon level employees (LaForge 2016). She also removed—with the help of a presidential decree—the powerful director generals of taxes and customs and excise that had blocked reform efforts in the past. To improve recruitment and morale, she raised salaries significantly by providing supplements (and despite resistance from MenPAN), created new standard operating procedures, and introduced a performance management system using a "balanced scorecard" (Budiarso 2016). She also actively supported anti-corruption efforts by collaborating with the anti-corruption commission (KPK) and reassigning problematic employees to low-risk positions (LaForge 2016). The experience of the Ministry of Finance illustrates the possibility for substantial reform and progress but also highlights several practical challenges, often tied to political resistance and interference, in implementing reforms.

Specific to human resources management, the new ministerial regulation MenPAN RB No. 3/2020 on Talent Management in the civil service directs all civil service units to develop their own tailored management strategy. It remains to be seen to what extent and speed various ministries and units will be able to draft and implement a comprehensive talent management plan.

A separate regulatory issue pertains to the legal status and future of contract employees in the civil service. The widespread past and current practice of hiring contract teachers in the education sector and the desire to convert them to official civil servant status has generated a need for further clarification with regard to the current and future role of contract employees. While Government Regulation No. 48/2005 details appointment procedures of past nonpermanent employees, the Civil Service Law No. 5/2014 introduced a new category of government employees with a work agreement (PPPK), which can be used to appoint professionals on a nonpermanent basis as state employees. Government Regulation No. 49/2018 provides further details on the recruitment, selection, and termination of government employees with a work agreement (PPPK). These new regulations have generated questions with respect to the application of age limits and civil service entry tests in the conversion of old contract employees into the new status categories.

Laws and regulations specifically aimed at corruption have also added to the regulatory framework of the civil service. Law No. 28/1999 for instance obliges all state administrators to swear an oath to abstain from all acts of corruption and be willing to disclose and have their financial assets investigated (Sondang Silitonga 2018). A series of laws have also established the Corruption Eradication Commission, its obligations and law enforcement authorities, specific crimes, and whistleblower statutes (Law No. 31/1999, Law No. 20/2001, Law No. 30/2002, Law No. 46/2009, Law No. 8/2010, Law No. 13/2006, Law No. 31/2014, and Presidential Regulation No. 87/2016). Enforcement of many of these statutes remains incomplete—e.g., assets disclosed by public officials in 2014 was only 28.3% (Sondang Silitonga 2018).

At the local level, the introduction of direct elections for the district head office seems to have slowed the progress of civil service reforms (Berenschot 2018; Blunt, Turner, and Lindroth 2012a, 2012b). The political importance of vote buying and related clientelistic strategies give district heads a strong incentive to establish control over state resources for leverage during election campaigns—and includes gaining the allegiance and support of civil servants and providing incentives for district heads to slow or block the application of merit principles in the management of the civil service (Berenschot 2018). Government Regulation No. 53/2010 explicitly prohibits supporting campaign activities of regional heads and mayors. Similarly, the 2016 Law on Regional Elections No. 10, reinforced by General Election Commission Regulation No. 2017/3, prohibits the transfer of civil servants by incumbent district heads 6 months before and after an election. Despite these regulatory efforts, civil servant participation in campaign activities remains widespread (Berenschot 2018), and transfers of civil servants during election periods occur despite explicit rules against it (Suwitri et al. 2019).

In sum, the Civil Service Reform Law of 2014 and subsequent regulations have moved the regulatory environment for a modernization of the civil service toward the right direction. Nonetheless, substantial hurdles for actual practical changes remain and often stem not only from a lack of political will but also from active resistance to reforms that limit or eliminate patronage and corruption opportunities.

Public Sector Performance, Corruption, and Clientelism

Reflecting the general institutional governance environment, Indonesia's civil service has had a mixed record of public service delivery over the last 20 years. Drawing on a number of different indicators of service delivery at the district level from the World Bank's INDO-DAPOER database,[9] Figures 4.2–4.7 illustrate secular improvements in 2001–2013. Figure 18 uses an average of the Services Provision Index[10] across district

---

9   World Bank. Indonesia Database for Policy and Economic Research (INDO-DAPOER). https://datacatalog.worldbank.org/dataset/indonesia-database-policy-and-economic-research

10 The Services Provision Index combines data on percentage of the population with safe access to sanitation, percentage of the population with safe access to water, school enrollment rates, percentage of births attended by skilled staff, and the quality of roads. Inputs are combined via covariance weighting.

governments. The figure reveals substantial overall increases in services over time. From 2001 to 2013 the average of the index increased from a low of −0.76 to a high of 2.03, which is equivalent to 75% of a standard deviation of the district-level index.

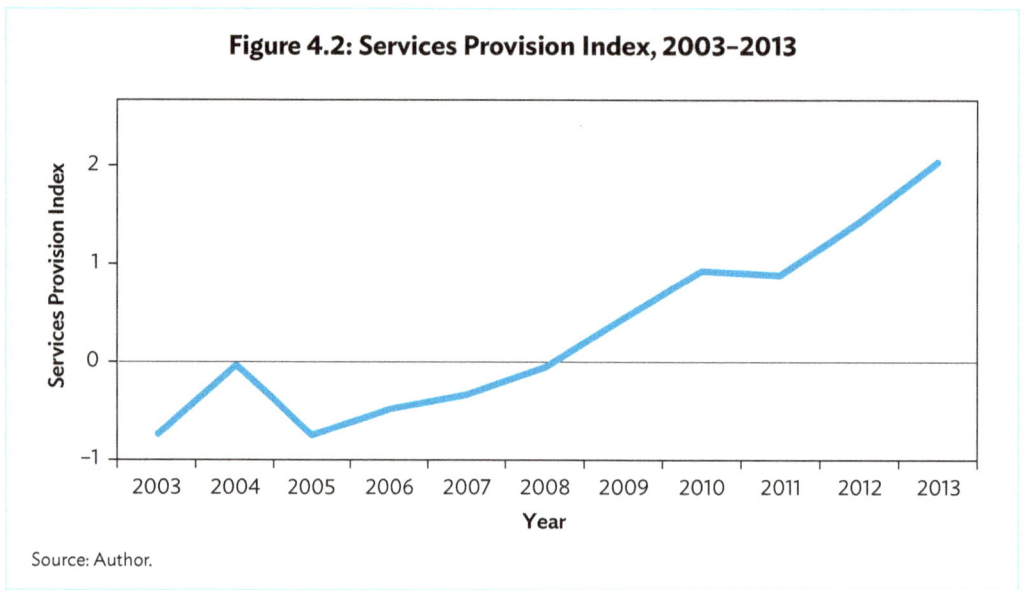

Figure 4.2: Services Provision Index, 2003–2013

Source: Author.

This overall increase is reflected in improvements across component categories (Figures 4.3–4.6). Across all indicators we observe at least some improvement in outcomes in 2001–2013.

Another holistic measure of government performance, poverty per capita, tells a similar story. Figure 4.7 shows continuous reduction in poverty across district governments.

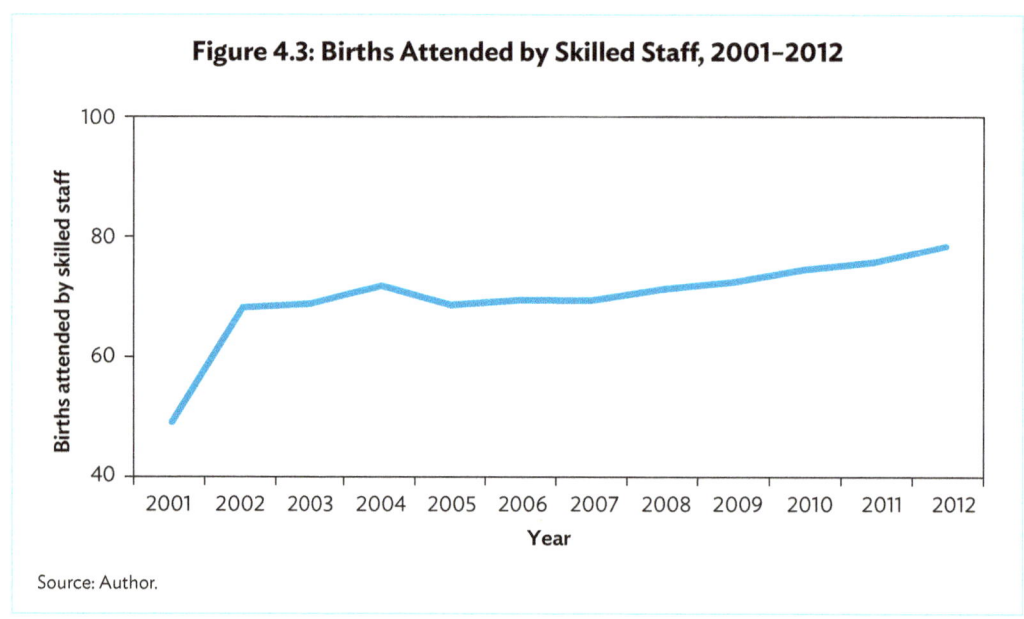

Figure 4.3: Births Attended by Skilled Staff, 2001–2012

Source: Author.

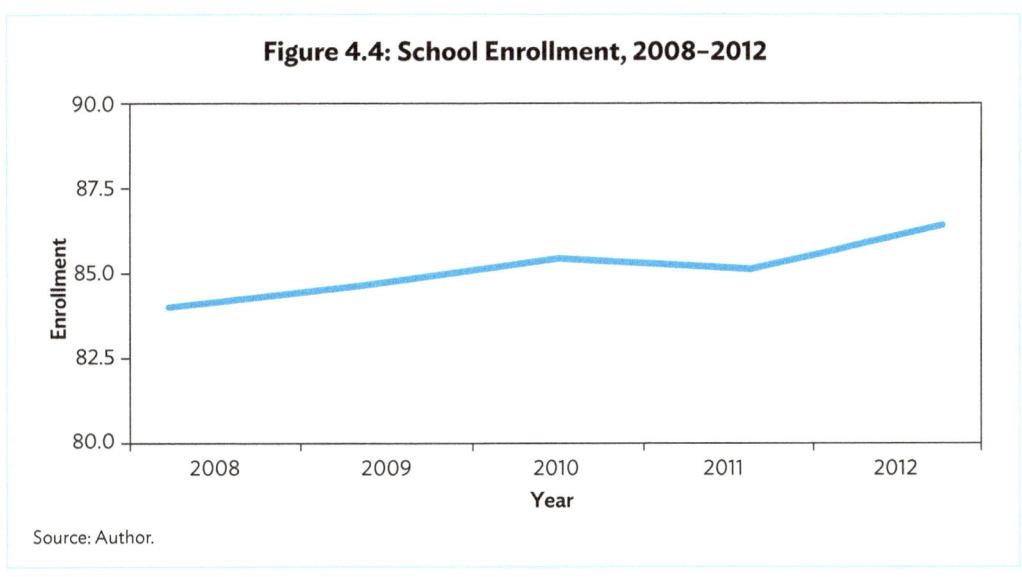
Figure 4.4: School Enrollment, 2008–2012

Source: Author.

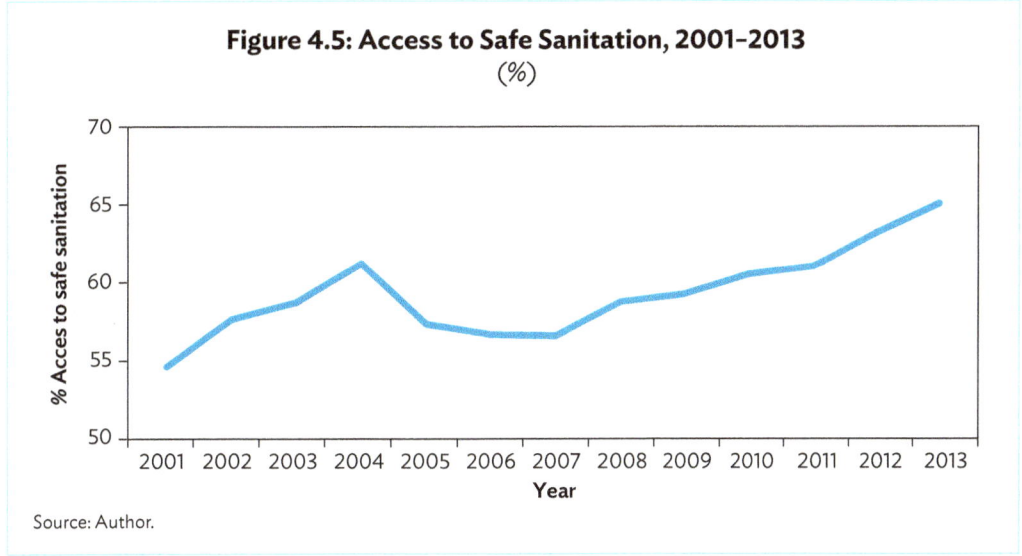
Figure 4.5: Access to Safe Sanitation, 2001–2013 (%)

Source: Author.

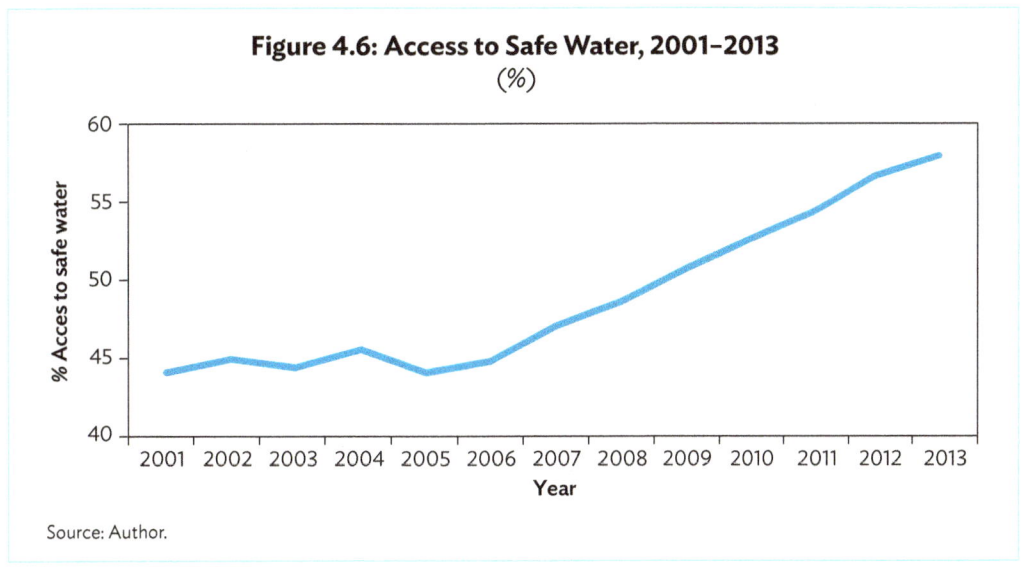
Figure 4.6: Access to Safe Water, 2001–2013 (%)

Source: Author.

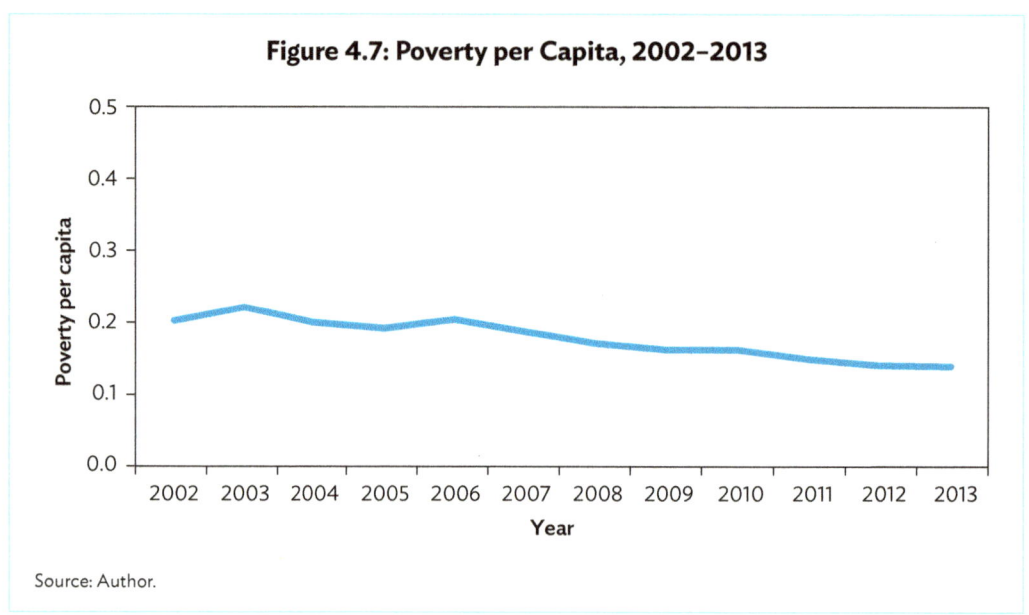

Figure 4.7: Poverty per Capita, 2002–2013

Source: Author.

Looking at Indonesian citizens' perception of public services, a less sanguine picture emerges. The Asian Barometer collected representative survey data for Indonesia in 2006, 2011, and 2016. The survey asked questions about access to public services, specifically to medical facilities, ID cards, police, and schools. Figure 4.8 displays the results of the survey with regard to the average degree of difficulty in accessing any of these services. On average, an overall picture of stability emerged: for all four services, respondents scored access to be somewhere between "difficult" and "easy," with access to police and schools scoring lower than medical clinics and ID cards.

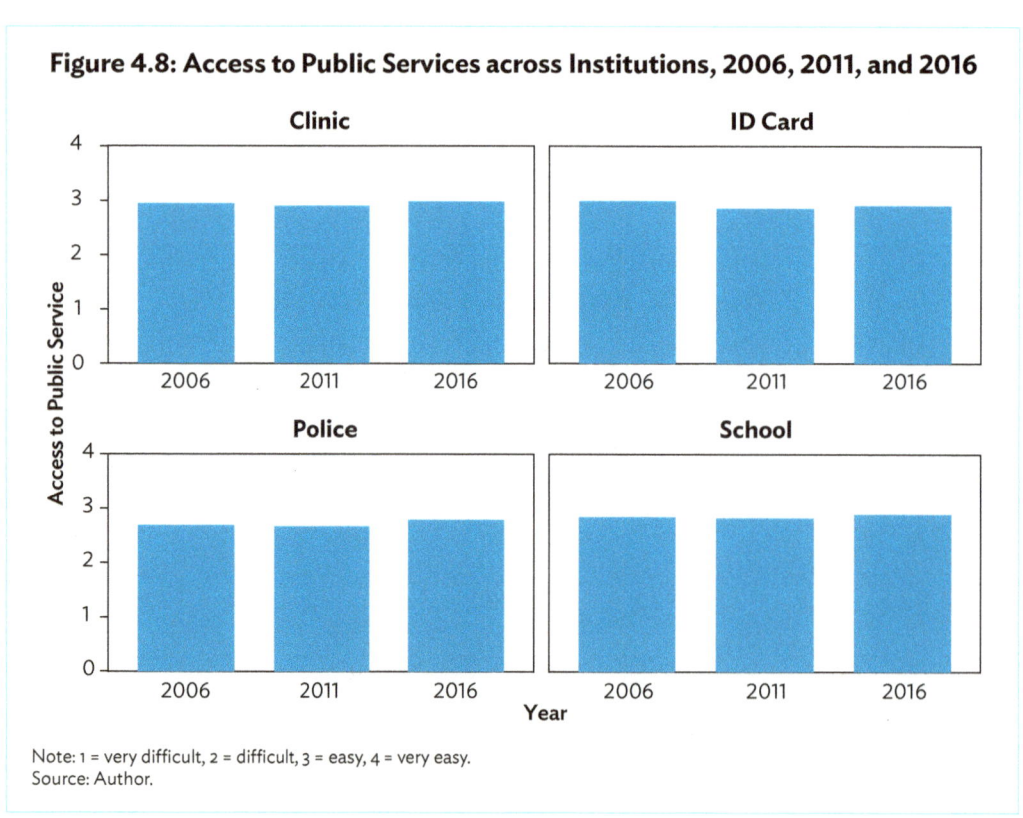

Figure 4.8: Access to Public Services across Institutions, 2006, 2011, and 2016

Note: 1 = very difficult, 2 = difficult, 3 = easy, 4 = very easy.
Source: Author.

In addition, the Asian Barometer survey also included questions on trust in specific government institutions. Figure 4.9 reports on the average levels of trust in the civil service, the courts, local government, the military, Parliament, and the police. Across all institutions, average responses are close to "3 – quite a lot," with Parliament scoring the lowest and the military scoring the highest (especially after 2006). In the case of temporal changes, the civil service is seen to have experienced a slight erosion in citizens' trust, whereas local governments and the military have enjoyed gains from 2006 to 2016. Figure 4.10 gives the same data but facilitates a comparison across institutions within the same period, indicating clearly that while the civil service was the most trusted institution in 2006, it lost that status by 2011 and 2016.

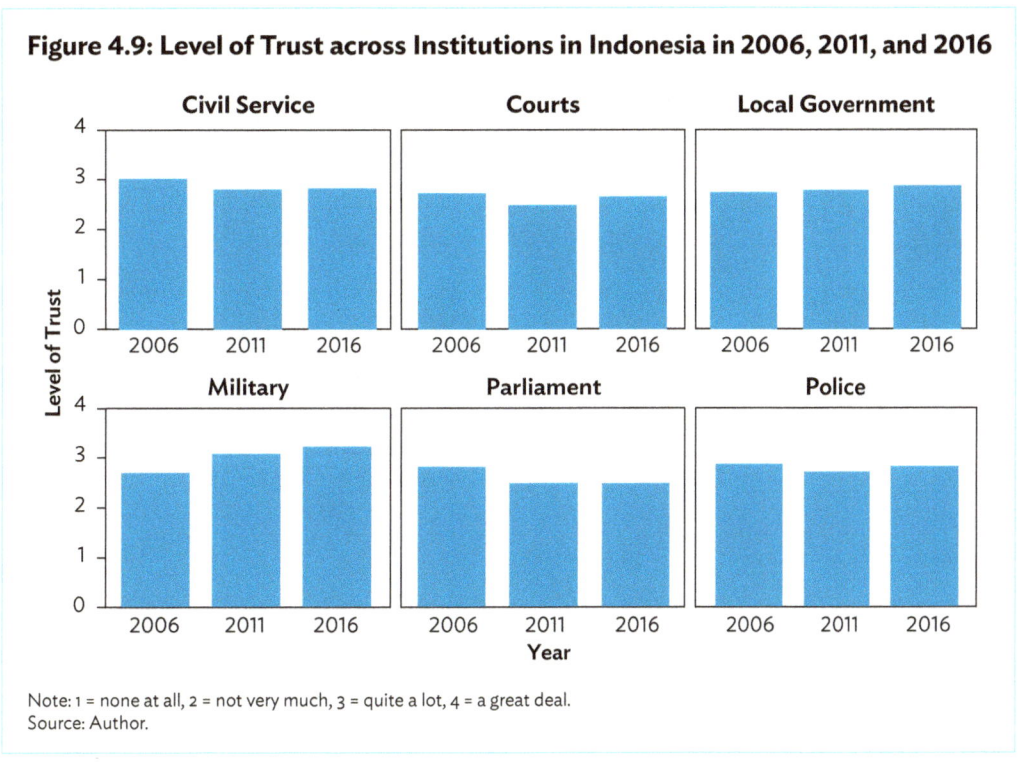

Figure 4.9: Level of Trust across Institutions in Indonesia in 2006, 2011, and 2016

Note: 1 = none at all, 2 = not very much, 3 = quite a lot, 4 = a great deal.
Source: Author.

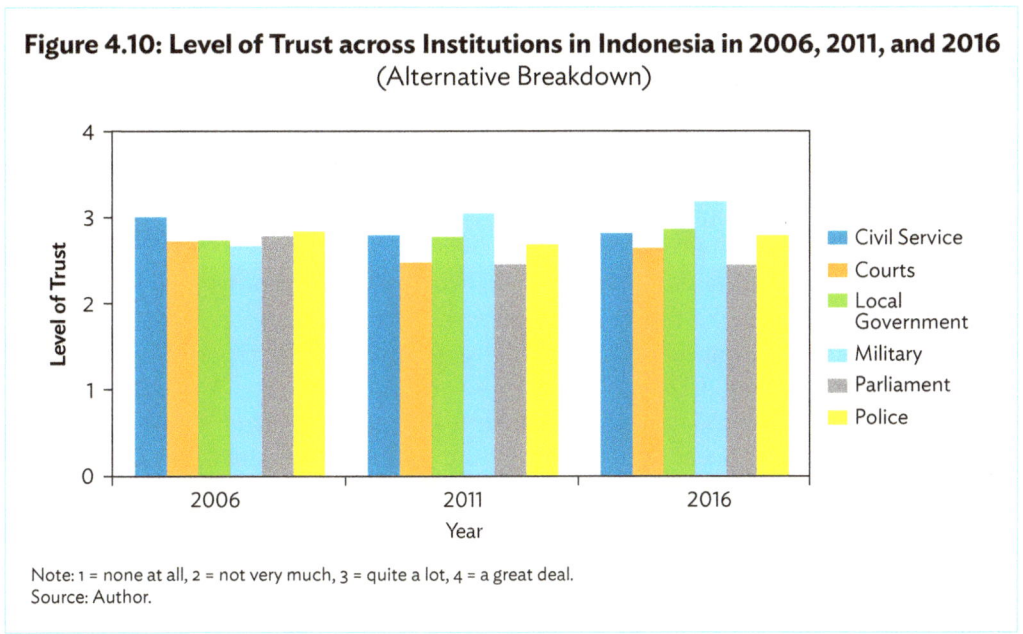

Figure 4.10: Level of Trust across Institutions in Indonesia in 2006, 2011, and 2016
(Alternative Breakdown)

Note: 1 = none at all, 2 = not very much, 3 = quite a lot, 4 = a great deal.
Source: Author.

The secular improvements in service delivery captured in Figures 4.2–4.7 also mask a wide variation in the quality of service delivery across districts. For example, Figure 4.11 shows the percentage of births attended by skilled staff across Indonesia. There exists a dramatic variation on this metric, ranging from under 20% in some regions (such as in parts of Papua) to over 80% in many districts of Java. This variation is indicative of the challenges generated for local civil service organizations as a consequence of decentralization reforms. While the reforms increased local accountability and the ability of local governments to tailor service delivery to the characteristics of their respective local population, it also reified resource inequities and generated a new politicization of the civil service at the local level.

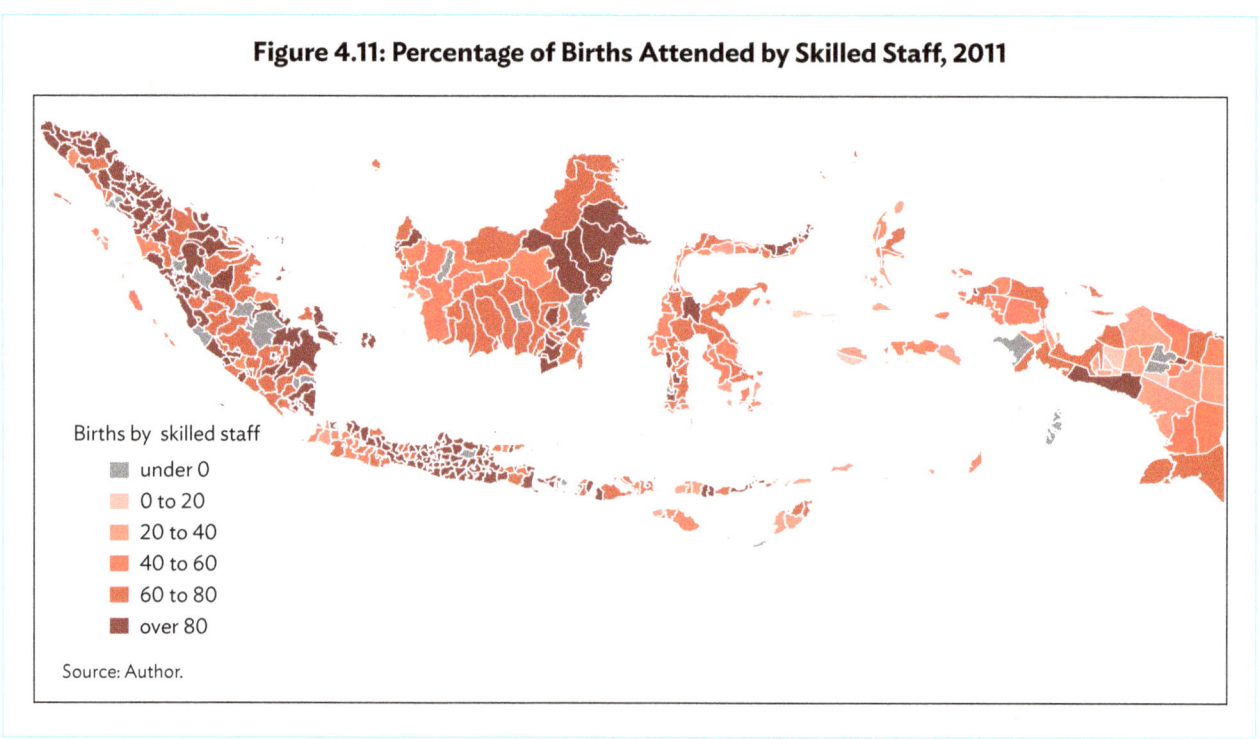

Figure 4.11: Percentage of Births Attended by Skilled Staff, 2011

Source: Author.

After the end of the Suharto regime in 1998, Indonesia introduced new forms of political accountability at the national and local levels and relocated authority for essential government services to the district level (Crouch 2010). To finance local governments' service delivery, the central government created a complex system of revenue-sharing and fiscal transfers (World Bank 2003). District government expenditures are financed largely through shared revenue allocations and block grants from the central government, while their local taxation authority as a revenue-generating source remains fairly limited (Lewis 2005).[11]

At the local level, district legislatures and district heads were given authority to author local budgets and vote on local laws and regulations, starting in 2001. Relative to local legislatures, the *bupati* or *walikota* (local district heads) have particularly important agenda-setting powers with respect to government spending. Initially district heads were selected by local legislatures, but in 2005, this indirect selection mechanism was replaced with direct elections. This electoral reform (i.e., the shift from indirect to direct elections) was driven by a general impression of elite collusion and a lack of transparency and accountability that was apparent in the indirect elections in which district head candidates had to be nominated by parties or coalitions of parties represented in local parliament, which often led to the selling of party nominations and

---

[11] The vast majority of district funds come from general transfers and natural resource revenues; only about 7% of district revenue is earmarked by the central government for specific expenditures.

votes to rich local candidates (Buehler 2010). While candidates are still required to secure party nominations in the current system,[12] bargaining in the legislature has been replaced by competitive general voting. This institutional change has created a competitive, albeit still elite-dominated, local electoral process (Erb and Sulistiyanto 2009).

Another important element of the decentralization reforms is the ability to create new district governments by splitting existing government units. This process of district proliferation dramatically increased the number of local governments and generated new challenges for the organization of local civil service units and the hiring of new staff (Pierskalla 2016; Lewis 2017).

While competitive local elections and the creation of smaller government units may generate incentives for local district heads to leverage their control over the civil service to improve service delivery, evidence does not seem to support this expectation. Several studies have investigated the effects of decentralization, local elections, and district creation on the performance of local governments. Kis-Katos and Sjahrir (2014) focus on administrative overspending and find that neither district-splitting nor the introduction of direct elections has meaningfully reduced the high levels of wasteful administrative expenditures. Nor do local elections seem to have substantive effects on sectoral investments in education, health care, or physical infrastructure (Kis-Katos and Sjahrir 2014). Skoufias et al. (2014) document that 4 years after the introduction of direct elections, no improvements in human development outcomes have been realized. Yet, at least in the area of health, per capita expenditures have increased in the wake of direct district head elections (Skoufias et al. 2014). With regard to political budget cycles, Sjahrir et al. (2013) show that discretionary administrative expenditures increase during election years, while Skoufias et al. (2014) find some evidence that sectoral or functional expenditures increase during election years. Pierskalla and Sacks (2019) document reductions to local infrastructure investments during election years. Lewis (2017) finds that the creation of new district governments did not improve school enrollment and had negative effects on infrastructure services.

Moreover, the expansive literature on the quality of Indonesian elections suggests that the introduction of direct elections in Indonesia has contributed to the emergence of mass-scale of clientelism and vote-buying (Aspinall and Berenschot 2019).

While clientelism and patronage were a constituent feature of the civil service under Suharto, it was a heavily centralized system of autocratic control, centered around Suharto and his immediate circle of cronies (McLeod 2008). After the fall of the Suharto regime, democratization contributed to the decentralization of the prior "franchise system" of corruption, which has led to intensified patronage politics, clientelism, and corruption overall (Aspinall and Berenschot 2019; Robison and Hadiz 2004; McLeod 2008; Blunt, Turner, and Lindroth 2012a, 2012b). This increase in election-related patronage also affects the civil service, where the leveraging of familial connections and the outright purchase of civil service positions is common (Kristiansen and Ramli 2006; Tidey 2012; Berenschot 2018; Blunt, Turner, and Lindroth 2012a, 2012b; Suwitri et al. 2019) and civil servants play an increasingly central role in electoral politics (Pierskalla and Sacks 2019; Aspinall and Berenschot 2019; Berenschot 2018).

Efforts to combat corruption have had mixed success. The general success of the Indonesian Anti-Corruption Commission (KPK) has unveiled a number of high-profile corruption incidents involving political actors and bureaucrats. However, recent reform efforts by the Widodo government and the national Parliament seem to seek to curtail the effectiveness of the KPK (Lindsey 2019). Efforts to rein in corruption at the local level have also been limited, in part due to the increased influence of district heads. A study which aimed to evaluate the effectiveness of various institutional mechanisms in reducing corruption in local development programs found evidence in support of more top–down control. Using a randomized controlled trial in comparing the

---

[12] Independent candidates are allowed, but the regulatory and financial burden is seen as prohibitively high.

effectiveness of top–down oversight via government audits versus grassroots participation of community members, Olken (2007) found substantial reductions in corruption via audits. Overall, data from Transparency International (Table 3.13) and Gallup World Poll reported by OECD and ADB (2019) (and reproduced in Figure 4.12), indicate no improvement in government corruption over the last 15 years.

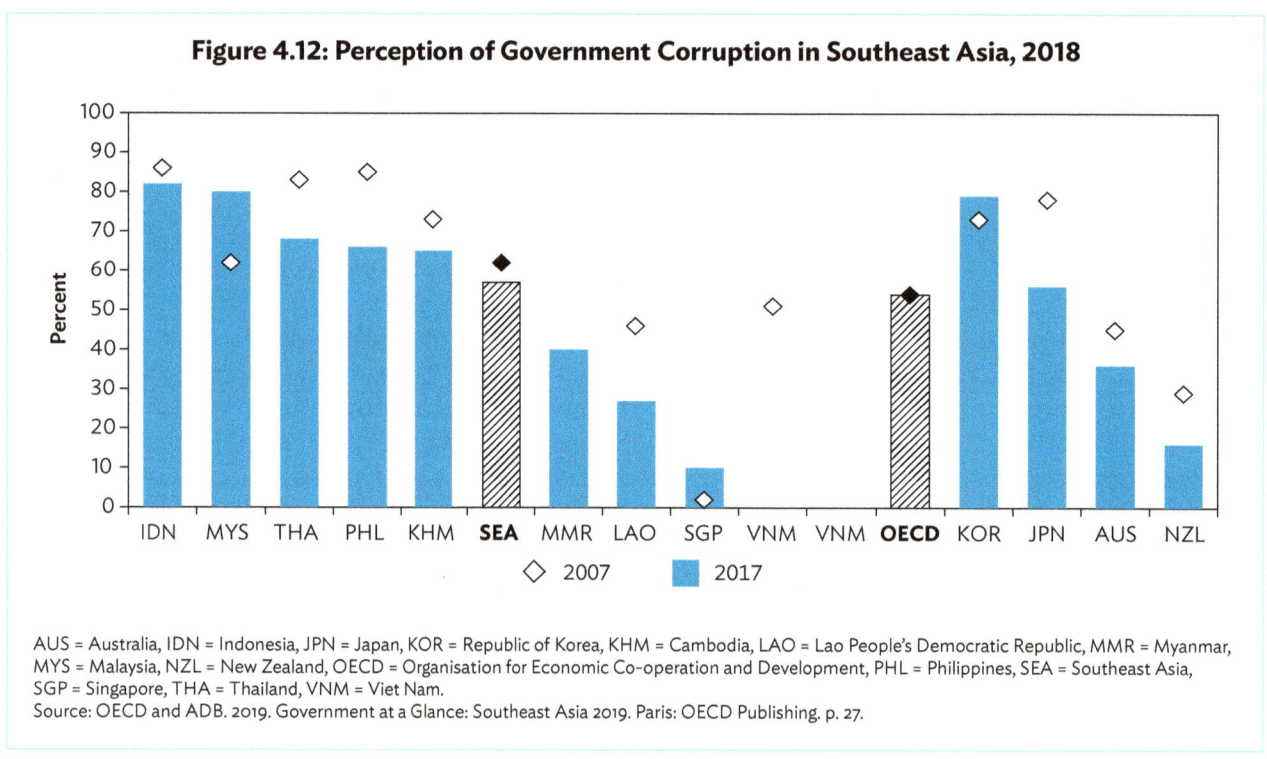

Figure 4.12: Perception of Government Corruption in Southeast Asia, 2018

AUS = Australia, IDN = Indonesia, JPN = Japan, KOR = Republic of Korea, KHM = Cambodia, LAO = Lao People's Democratic Republic, MMR = Myanmar, MYS = Malaysia, NZL = New Zealand, OECD = Organisation for Economic Co-operation and Development, PHL = Philippines, SEA = Southeast Asia, SGP = Singapore, THA = Thailand, VNM = Viet Nam.
Source: OECD and ADB. 2019. Government at a Glance: Southeast Asia 2019. Paris: OECD Publishing. p. 27.

In sum, improving the Indonesian civil service writ large requires a serious commitment to address governance challenges. Overlapping hierarchies and unclear responsibilities across levels of government constrain the central government's efforts in internal monitoring and its ability to steer the civil service. At the local level, the nature of electoral competition in Indonesia seems to have exacerbated the role of clientelism and corruption, making the civil service a valuable target for political interference.

5. RECOMMENDATIONS AND CONCLUSION

This report provided a broad overview of the key issues facing Indonesia's civil service. Drawing on various data sources and secondary literature, the report highlights several issues:

1. The structure of the Indonesian civil service replicates many features of bureaucracies around the world in terms of its internal organization, size, pay structure, and basic rules of operation.

2. The national average indicators of the civil service's size and diversity and the competence and performance of civil servants mask a wide spatial variation across the geography of Indonesia. Spatial inequality across provincial and district government civil service organizations is large, as seen in terms of sheer size; the levels of educational attainment and professionalism of civil servants; the availability of a specialized, technical workforce in, for example the medical field; gender imbalances; projected retirements, and the quality of service delivery. Reducing spatial inequities in the Indonesian civil service will be an important challenge going forward.

3. In skills and competency, Indonesian civil servants overall demonstrate lower than expected levels of educational attainment, which vary for the most part across the levels of government and across regional government units. The government's own Professionalism Index classifies a large part of the civil service as being of "low" quality.

4. It is unclear to what extent existing recruiting practices and on-the-job training programs address the current and future needs of Indonesia's civil service, as a comprehensive assessment of skills and planning for future needs across all government units has yet to be done.

5. The education sector exemplifies many of the ongoing challenges to improve governance in Indonesia. Despite the well-intentioned reforms and an influx of fiscal resources into the education sector, Indonesian schools have not shown much improvement in the quality of service delivery. Instead, reform efforts have led to a substantial increase in the teaching workforce, especially of contract teachers, and in teacher salary increases.

6. Historically, gender diversity in the Indonesian civil service has been lacking. While the civil service employs roughly the same number of men and women overall, women are underrepresented in leadership positions. The career penalty for women has also been increasing since democratization and decentralization in 1999 and 2001, respectively. These will likely have important implications for the quality of service delivery and the broader population's perceptions of the civil service.

7. Administrative data are collected and available, but these are not standardized and used adequately in policy-making decisions. Meanwhile, data gaps exist and a fragmented human resources system gives rise to a need for better supervision, oversight, and to leverage the potential of digital technology.

8. The Indonesian civil service also faces significant governance challenges. While a modernized regulatory framework, decentralization, and the creation of many new district governments have brought forth opportunities for change and improvements in service delivery, reforms have also created new challenges. The central government has limited oversight and capacity to steer developments at the local level. Decentralization and local elections have generated incentives for increased corruption and given rise to the politicization of the civil service especially during electoral efforts of politicians. This has slowed down or outright hindered the enforcement of national regulations meant to foster merit principles.

REFERENCES

Aspinall, E. and W. Berenschot. 2019. *Democracy for Sale. Elections, Clientelism, and the State in Indonesia.* Ithaca, NY: Cornell University Press.

Azmi, I., A. G., S. H. S. Ismail, and S. A. Basir. 2012. Women Career Advancement in Public Service: A Study in Indonesia. *Procedia – Social and Behavioral Sciences.* 58. pp. 298–306.

Banuri, S. and P. Keefer. 2016. Pro-Social Motivation, Effort and the Call to Public Service. *European Economic Review.* 83. pp. 139–164.

Barnes, T. D., E. Beaulieu, and G. W. Saxton. 2018. Restoring Trust in the Police: Why Female Officers Reduce Suspicions of Corruption. *Governance.* 31 (1). pp. 143–161.

Berenschot, W. 2018. Incumbent Bureaucrats: Why Elections Undermine Civil Service Reform in Indonesia. *Public Administration & Development.* 38. pp. 135–143.

Besley, T. and M. Reynal-Querol. 2011. Do Democracies Select More Educated Leaders?. *American Political Science Review.* 105 (3). pp. 552–566.

Besley, T., O. Folke, T. Persson, and J. Rickne. 2017. Gender Quotas and the Crisis of the Mediocre Man: Theory and Evidence from Sweden. *American Economic Review.* 107 (8). pp. 2204–2242.

Bhavnani, R. R. and A. Lee. 2019. Does Affirmative Action Worsen Bureaucratic Performance? Evidence from the Indian Administrative Service. *American Journal of Political Science.* https://onlinelibrary.wiley.com/doi/abs/10.1111/ajps.12497.

Badan Kepegawaian Negara (BKN). 2018. Civil Servant Statistics Book December 2018. Jakarta.

Badan Kepegawaian Negara (BKN). 2019. Results Report. Professionality Index Measurement, State Civil Apparatus, 2018. Jakarta.

Blunt, P., M. Turner, and H. Lindroth. 2012a. Patronage, Service Delivery, and Social Justice in Indonesia. *International Journal of Public Administration.* 35 (2). pp. 214–2020.

Blunt, P., M. Turner, and H. Lindroth. 2012b. Patronage's Progress in Post-Suharto Indonesia. *Public Administration and Development.* 32. pp. 64–81.

Budiarso, A. 2016. Improving Government Performance in Indonesia: The Experience of the Balanced Scorecard in The Ministry of Finance. Doctoral Dissertation, University of Canberra. http://www.canberra.edu.au/researchrepository/file/1a2c8cf2-bdca-47bd-86d5-674f3a216b70/1/full_text.pdf.

Bradbury, M. and J. E. Kellough. 2011. Representative Bureaucracy: Assessing the Evidence on Active Representation. *The American Review of Public Administration.* 41 (2). pp. 157–167.

Brollo, F. and U. Troiano. 2016. What Happens When a Woman Wins an Election? Evidence from Close Races in Brazil. *Journal of Development Economics.* 122. pp. 28–45.

Buehler, M. 2010. Decentralisation and Local Democracy in Indonesia: The Marginalisation of the Public Sphere. In E. Aspinall and M. Mietzner, eds. *Problems of Democratisation in Indonesia: Elections, Institutions and Society.* Singapore: ISEAS.

Card, D. 1999. The Causal Effect of Education on Earnings. *Handbook of Labor Economics.* 3. pp. 1801–1863.

Cerdan-Infantes, P., Y. Makarova, S. Al-Samarrai, and D. Chen. 2013. Spending More or Spending Better: Improving Education Financing in Indonesia. World Bank Report. http://documents.worldbank.org/curated/en/2013/03/17537371/spending-more-or-spending-better-improving-education-financing-indonesia

Chang, M. C., S. Shaeffer, S. Al-Samarrai, A. B. Ragatz, and J. de Ree. 2013. Teacher Reform in Indonesia: The Role of Politics and Evidence in Policy Making, World Bank Report. http://documents.worldbank.org/curated/en/2013/11/18606227/teacher-reform-indonesia-role-politics-evidence-policy-making

Chin, A. and N. Prakash. 2011. The Redistributive Effects of Political Reservation for Minorities: Evidence from India. *Journal of Development Economics.* 96 (2). pp. 265–277.

Clayton, A. and P. Zetterberg. 2018. Quota Shocks: Electoral Gender Quotas and Government Spending Priorities Worldwide. *The Journal of Politics.* 80 (3). pp. 916–932.

Crouch, H. 2010. *Political Reform in Indonesia after Soeharto.* Singapore: ISEAS.

De Ree, J., K. Muralidharan, M. Pradhan, and H. Rogers. 2018. Double for Nothing? Experimental Evidence on an Unconditional Teacher Salary Increase in Indonesia. *Quarterly Journal of Economics.* 133 (2). pp. 993–1039.

Duflo, E. 2012. Women Empowerment and Economic Development. *Journal of Economic Literature.* 50 (4). pp. 1051–1079.

Dwiputrianti, S. 2018. Challenges with Implementation of the Merit System in the Open Recruitment of Government High Positions: The Case of Indonesia. *Advances in Social Science, Education and Humanities Research.* 191.

Erb, M. and P. Sulistiyanto, eds. 2009. *Deepening Democracy in Indonesia? Direct Elections for Local Leaders (Pilkada).* Singapore: ISEAS.

Evans, P. and J. E. Rauch. 1999. Bureaucracy and Growth: A Cross-National Analysis of the Effects of "Weberian" State Structures on Economic Growth. *American Sociological Review.* 64 (5). pp. 748–765.

Ferraz, C. and F. Finan. 2009. Motivating Politicians: The Impacts of Monetary Incentives on Quality and Performance. *NBER Working Paper.* 14906. https://www.nber.org/papers/w14906.

Finan, F., B. Olken, and R. Pande. 2015. The Personnel Economics of the State. NBER Working Paper. 21825.

Gulzar, S., N. Haas, and B. Pasquale. 2018. Representation and Development across Groups: Evidence from a Large-Scale Government Program in India. Working Paper No. 1043. Stanford Center on Global Poverty and Development. https://kingcenter.stanford.edu/sites/default/files/publications/1043wp_0319.pdf

Hasnain, Z., N. Manning, and J. Pierskalla. 2014. The Promise of Performance Pay? Reasons for Caution in Policy Prescriptions in the Core Civil Service. *World Bank Research Observer.* 29 (2). pp. 235–264.

He, G. and S. Wang. 2017. Do College Graduates Serving as Village Officials Help Rural China?. *American Economic Journal: Applied Economics.* 9 (4). pp. 186–215.

Herring, C. 2009. Does Diversity Pay? Race, Gender, and the Business Case for Diversity. *American Sociological Review.* 74 (2). pp. 208–224.

International Civil Service Effectiveness Index (InCiSE). 2019. The International Civil Service Effectiveness Index—Results Report 2019. https://www.bsg.ox.ac.uk/about/partnerships/international-civil-service-effectiveness-index-2019.

Jakarta Post. 2018. Govt Looks to Private Employees to Fill Public Jobs After 90% of Applicants Fail Basic Test. https://www.thejakartapost.com/news/2018/11/18/govt-looks-to-private-employees-to-fill-public-jobs-after-90-percent-of-applicants-fail-basic-skills-test.html.

Kis-Katos, K. and B. S. Sjahrir. 2014. The Impact of Fiscal and Political Decentralization on Local Public Investments in Indonesia. IZA Discussion Paper No. 7884. Bonn, Germany.

Krislov, S. 2012. *Representative Bureaucracy.* New Orleans, LA: Quid Pro Books.

Kristiansen, S. and M. Ramli. 2006. Buying an Income: The Market for Civil Service Positions in Indonesia. *Contemporary Southeast Asia: A Journal of International and Strategic Affairs.* 28 (2). pp. 207–233.

Krissetyanti, E. P. L., E. Prasojo, and A. Kasim. 2017. Meritocracy and Gender Equity: Opportunity for Women Civil Service to Occupy the High Leader Position in Local Bureaucracy in Indonesia. *Advances in Social Science, Education and Humanities Research.* 167.

LaForge, G. 2016. Changing a Civil Service Culture: Reforming Indonesia's Ministry of Finance, 2006–2010. Innovations for Successful Societies Case Study. https://successfulsocieties.princeton.edu/publications/changing-civil-service-culture-indonesia-finance-ministry.

Levi, M. and A. Sacks. 2009. Legitimating Beliefs: Sources and Indicators. *Regulation & Governance.* 3 (4). pp. 311–333.

Lewis, B. D. 2005. Indonesian Local Government Spending, Taxing and Saving: An Explanation of Pre- and Post-decentralization Fiscal Outcomes. *Asian Economic Journal.* 19. pp. 291–317.

Lewis, B. D. 2017. Does Local Government Proliferation Improve Public Service Delivery? Evidence from Indonesia. *Journal of Urban Affairs.* 39 (8). pp. 1047–1065.

Lindsey, T. 2019. A Requiem for Reformasi as Joko Widodo Unravels Indonesia's Democratic Legacy. *The Conversation.* http://theconversation.com/a-requiem-for-reformasi-as-joko-widodo-unravels-indonesias-democratic-legacy-125295.

Martinez-Bravo, M. 2017. The Local Political Economy Effects of School Construction in Indonesia. *American Economic Journal: Applied Economics.* 9 (2). pp. 256–289.

McLeod, R. H. 2000. Soeharto's Indonesia: A Better Class of Corruption. *Agenda: A Journal of Policy Analysis and Reform.* 7 (2). pp. 99–112.

McLeod, R. H. 2008. Inadequate Budgets and Salaries as Instruments for Institutionalizing Public Sector Corruption in Indonesia. *South East Asia Research.* 16 (2). pp. 199–223.

Mettler, S. 1998. *Dividing Citizens: Gender and Federalism in the New Deal Public Policy.* Ithaca, NY: Cornell University Press.

Nuswantoro, H. 2017. Does the Implementation of a Formal Performance Management System Improve Employee Performance? Perspectives from Indonesian Civil Servants. MA thesis, University of Melbourne. https://tinyurl.com/s3ukt9v

OECD. 2017. Skills for a High Performing Civil Service. OECD Public Governance Reviews. https://www.oecd.org/gov/skills-for-a-high-performing-civil-service-9789264280724-en.htm.

OECD and ADB. 2019. *Government at a Glance Southeast Asia 2019.* Paris: OECD Publishing. https://doi.org/10.1787/9789264305915-en.

Olken, B. 2007. Monitoring Corruption: Evidence from a Field Experiment in Indonesia. *Journal of Political Economy.* 115 (2). pp. 200–249.

Pande, R. 2003. Can Mandated Political Representation Increase Policy Influence for Disadvantaged Minorities? Theory and Evidence from India. *American Economic Review.* 93 (4). pp. 1132–1151.

Park, S. 2013. Does Gender Matter? The Effect of Gender Representation of Public Bureaucracy on Governmental Performance. *The American Review of Public Administration.* 43 (2). pp. 221–242.

Pepinsky, T. B., J. Pierskalla, and A. Sacks. 2017. Bureaucracy and Service Delivery. *Annual Review of Political Science.* 20. pp. 249–268.

Pierskalla, J. H. 2016. Splitting the Difference? The Politics of District Creation in Indonesia. *Comparative Politics.* 48 (2). pp. 249–268.

Pierskalla, J. H. and A. Sacks. 2019. Personnel Politics: Elections, Clientelistic Competition and Teacher Hiring in Indonesia. *British Journal of Political Science.* 50 (4). pp. 1283–1305.

Pierskalla, J. H., A. Lauretig, A. S. Rosenberg, and A. Sacks. 2019. Democratization and Representative Bureaucracy – An Analysis of Promotion Patterns in Indonesia's Civil Service, 1980–2015. *American Journal of Political Science.*

Pierskalla, J. 2019. Competence and Control: The Effect of Democratization on the Civil Service. Working Paper.

Rasul, I. and D. Rogger. 2015. The Impact of Ethnic Diversity in Bureaucracies: Evidence from the Nigerian Civil Service. *American Economic Review.* 105 (5). pp. 457–461.

Rauch, J. E. and P. Evans. 2000. Bureaucratic Structure and Bureaucratic Performance in Less Developed Countries. *Journal of Public Economics.* 75 (1). pp. 49–71.

Reformasi Weekly. 2019. Issues 1–11. 2019.

Riccucci, N. M., G. G. Van Ryzin, and C. F. Lavena. 2014. Representative Bureaucracy in Policing: Does It Increase Perceived Legitimacy?. *Journal of Public Administration Research and Theory.* 24 (3). pp. 537–551.

Robison, R. and V. Hadiz. 2004. *Reorganising Power in Indonesia. The Politics of Oligarchy in an Age of Markets.* London: Routledge.

Rogger, D. 2017. Who Serves the Poor? Surveying Civil Servants in the Developing World. Policy Research Working Paper. 8051. Washington, DC: World Bank. http://documents.worldbank.org/curated/en/152091493913163207/pdf/WPS8051.pdf.

Shair-Rosenfield, S. 2012. The Alternative Incumbency Effect: Electing Women Legislators in Indonesia. *Electoral Studies.* 31 (3). pp. 576–587.

Sjahrir, B. S., K. Kis-Katos, and G. Schulze. 2013. Political Budget Cycles in Indonesia at the District Level. *Economics Letters.* 120 (2). pp. 342–45.

Skoufias, E., A. Narayan, B. Dasgupta, and K. Kaiser. 2014. Electoral Accountability and Local Government Spending in Indonesia. Policy Research Working Paper. No. 5614. Washington, DC: World Bank.

Sondang Silitonga, M. 2018. *Corruption in Indonesia: The Impact of Institutional Change, Norms, and Networks.* Groningen: University of Groningen.

Suwitri, S., B. Supriyono, S. Sulastri, and O. Kuswandaru. 2019. Transactional Politics in Filling High Leadership Positions in Indonesian Bureaucratic Organizations. *International Journal of Research in Humanities and Social Studies.* 6 (5). pp. 38–50.

Tendler, J. and S. Freedheim. 1994. Trust in a Rent-Seeking World: Health and Government Transformed in Northeast Brazil. *World Development.* 22 (12).1 pp. 771–1791.

Theobald, N. A. and D. P. Haider-Markel. 2009. Race, Bureaucracy, and Symbolic Representation: Interactions between Citizens and Police. *Journal of Public Administration Research and Theory.* 19 (2). pp. 409–426.

Tidey, S. 2012. Performing the State. Everyday Practices, Corruption and Reciprocity in Middle Indonesian Civil Service. Dissertation, University of Amsterdam.

Tjiptoherijanto, P. 2007. Civil Service Reform in Indonesia. *International Public Management Review.* 8 (2). pp. 31–44.

Tjiptoherijanto, P. 2014. Reform of the Indonesian Civil Service: Racing with Decentralization. Working Paper in Economics and Business, Department of Economics. http://econ.feb.ui.ac.id/wp-content/uploads/2015/10/201402.pdf

Tjiptoherijanto, P. 2018. Reform of the Indonesian Civil Service: Looking for Quality. *Economics World.* 6 (6). pp. 433–443.

United Nations (UN) Women. 2015. *Progress of the World's Women 2015–2016: Transforming Economies, Realizing Rights.* Milan. http://progress.unwomen.org/en/2015/pdf/UNW_progressreport.pdf

Vernby, K. 2013. Inclusion and Public Policy: Evidence from Sweden's Introduction of Noncitizen Suffrage. *American Journal of Political Science.* 57 (1). pp. 15–29.

Weaver, J. 2020. Jobs for Sale: Corruption and Misallocation in Hiring. Working Paper. https://papers.ssrn.com/sol3/papers.cfm?abstract_id=3590721.

World Bank. 2003. Decentralizing Indonesia: A Regional Public Expenditure Review. Report no. 26191. Washington, DC: World Bank Group.

World Bank. 2018a. Reforming Civil Service Recruitment through Computerized Examinations in Indonesia. Case Study from the Global Report on Improving Public Sector Performance. http://documents.worldbank.org/curated/en/833041539871513644/122290272_201811348033538/additional/131020-WP-P163620-WorldBankGlobalReport-PUBLIC.pdf.

Sacks, A. and J. H. Pierskalla. 2018. *Mapping Indonesia's Civil Service.* Washington, DC: World Bank Group. http://documents.worldbank.org/curated/en/643861542638957994/Mapping-Indonesia-s-Civil-Service.

Wright, L. and V. Crockett Tellei. 1993. Women in Management in Indonesia. *International Studies of Management & Organization.* 23 (4). pp. 19–45.